Haynes
Digital Video
Manual

© Haynes Publishing 2004

Published by: Haynes Publishing
Sparkford, Yeovil, Somerset BA22 7JJ
Tel: 01963 442030 Fax: 01963 440001
Int. tel: +44 1963 442030 Fax: +44 1963 440001
E-mail: sales@haynes.co.uk
Website: www.haynes.co.uk

British Library Cataloguing in Publication Data:
A catalogue record for this book is available from the British Library

ISBN 1 84425 126 8

Printed in Britain by J. H. Haynes & Co. Ltd, Sparkford

Throughout this book, trademarked names are used. Rather than put a
trademark symbol after every occurrence of a trademarked name, we use
the names in an editorial fashion only, and to the benefit of the trademark
owner, with no intention of infringement of the trademark. Where such
designations appear in this book, they have been printed with initial caps.

Whilst we at J. H. Haynes & Co. Ltd strive to ensure the accuracy and
completeness of the information in this manual, it is provided entirely at the
risk of the user. Neither the company nor the author can accept liability for
any errors, omissions or damage resulting therefrom. In particular, users
should be aware that component and accessory manufacturers, and
software providers, can change specifications without notice, thus
appropriate professional advice should always be sought.

Haynes
Digital Video
Manual

A practical introduction to making
professional-looking home movies

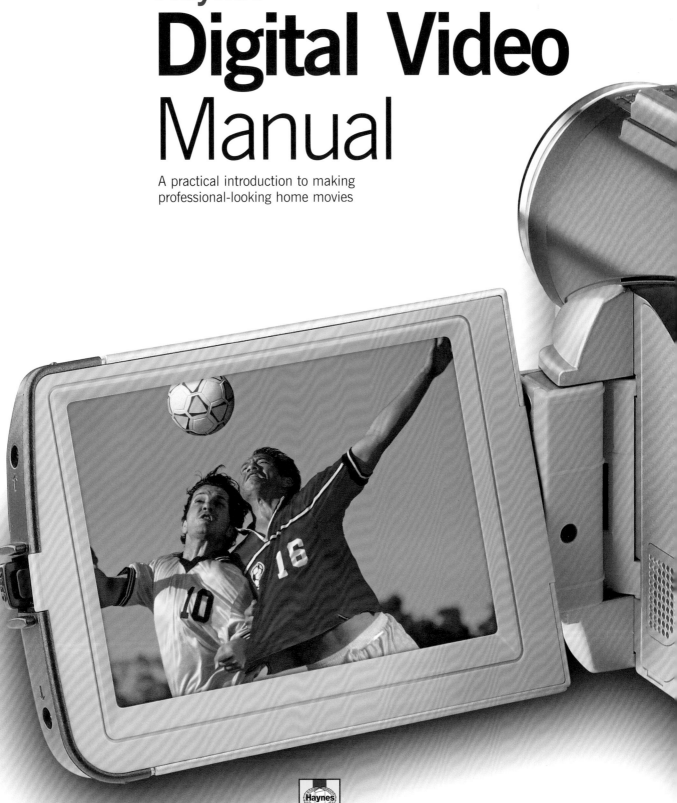

Haynes Publishing

Contents

Introduction

If you remember your parents setting up a projector in the living room on a Saturday night and beaming home movies onto a white tablecloth pinned to the wall -- or if indeed you are those parents – then digital video is going to come as something of a shock. Armed with only a digital camcorder and a computer, it is now both possible and ridiculously easy to shoot and produce professional-looking movies.

And, importantly, to share them.

Four steps to Hollywood

Indeed, digital video is one area of modern computing (the only area, perhaps?) where reality actually exceeds the hype. In our experience, subject to just one caveat, nobody is ever disappointed with a digital camcorder. On the contrary, most of us are startled to discover just how satisfying and rewarding it is making movies on a PC. The technology may be fearsomely complex behind the scenes but the hands-on practicalities are a cinch:

1 Point your camcorder at something worth shooting

2 Copy the footage onto your computer

A digital camcorder is small, light, immensely powerful and a great deal of fun.

3 Turn it into a polished movie with video editing software

4 Decide how to showcase your efforts.

The caveat we mentioned is that you need a powerful computer to work with digital video. Or rather you need a powerful computer to work with digital video at anything approaching an acceptable speed. While you can, of course, attempt to edit video on a low-spec system, we warn you now that you'll find it frustrating to the point of dejection. We cover the requirements in Part 1.

With video editing software and a beefy PC, you can work miracles with raw camcorder footage.

Number crunching

A widescreen TV is a better bet than a tablecloth these days but the real development in home movie-making lies more at the editing stage. This is the area we will concentrate on most in this manual. You no longer need regard your raw camcorder footage as the finished article, nor apologise during playback for all the bloopers, blunders and boring bits.

The beauty of working with digital video is that you can harness your computer's processing power to turn even the flakiest footage into something worth watching. If you've ever been impressed by the ways in which a PC can enhance a digital image, wait until you see what it can do with digital video.

With this book, you will learn how to:

- Organise and manipulate video as self-contained clips
- Apply scene transitions
- Add captions, titles and credits
- Work with still images
- Perform special cuts
- Use special effects
- Record a spoken narration

…and, of course, produce a DVD. We'll even help you choose a camcorder in the first place and offer a few sage tips about how to shoot good footage.

From digital camcorder to DVD…

The final cut

Any book on a subject as broad and detailed as digital video is necessarily an exercise in selection. But rather than skipping important subjects, our approach has been to dispense with as much of the jargon as possible. A video geek might scoff that there's no mention of I-, B- and P- frames or any explanation of MPEG GOP structures, but what would this add to your real-world experience? How much history on the diverse development of the MPEG-4 video format could you stomach before cottoning on that it wasn't actually getting you anywhere? Would a 50-page analysis of codecs and format conversions help you make a better movie?

Our goal was to write a guide to digital video that is, above all, practical. Our hope is that it will help you use a digital camcorder in a rewarding, fruitful and thoroughly enjoyable manner right from the off. Our expectation is that you'll be hooked for life.

Preserve your memories forever.

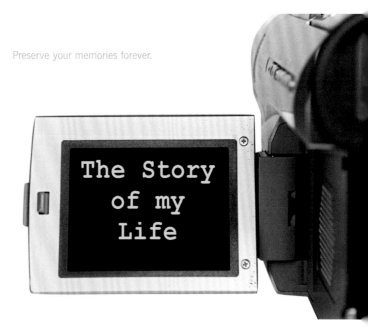

PART **1** # Hardware and software

Digital vs analogue (game over)

As no doubt you will have noticed, this is a guide to digital video written primarily for owners of digital camcorders. While it's true that much of what we discuss applies equally to analogue video – for instance, you can edit analogue source footage on a PC, produce polished movies and burn DVDs – we have no doubt whatsoever that digital is the way to go for anybody just setting out in this exciting field.

There are several reasons why in this context digital is better:

● **Digital camcorders and computers are complementary.** By which we mean that it's possible – in fact, straightforward to the point of simplicity – to transfer, or 'capture', footage from a digital camcorder onto a computer's hard drive. Because the source footage is essentially a bunch of binary data (1s and 0s), what you end up with on the hard drive is a perfect and precise copy of the original. The one pre-requisite is that your PC must have a FireWire interface, which we'll come to shortly.

It is of course possible to capture footage from an analogue camcorder or any other analogue video source such as a VCR, but you'll need a video capture card. This in itself is no great handicap and opens up all sorts of possibilities. For example, you might convert your old wedding videos to DVD. However, the source video has to go through an analogue-to-digital conversion in order to get on to your computer's hard drive, and the success of this process (i.e. the quality of the resultant digital video) depends on your hardware and software configuration. This needn't worry you if your goal is the one-off preservation of a wedding video but it's an issue you can do without when making home movies on a regular basis.

If your computer doesn't have an analogue video capture card, you can use an external breakout box like this one to capture video from a VCR or an analogue camcorder.

Digital camcorders are cool. They can also be very, very small.

- **Digital video is higher quality.** While professional-level analogue camcorders and film cameras produce broadcast-quality video, there's no real comparison between analogue and digital camcorders at the amateur or enthusiast level. The footage you shoot on even a basic digital camcorder is going to look better than the equivalent footage shot on an analogue camcorder at anything like a similar price point.

- **Digital camcorders are smaller, lighter, sexier, ...** No two ways about it: manufacturers invest a great deal of effort in making camcorders as user-friendly as possible, and the bulk of the effort in recent years has been focused on digital models. If you want a lightweight but fully-featured camcorder that you can take with you anywhere and use to shoot the most superb footage, digital is the way to go.

This Hi-8 camcorder is as good as it gets in the analogue arena.

Recording directly to (mini) DVD is an alternative to using tape.

Lightweight and no bigger than a pack of cards, this camcorder uses built-in memory rather than tape or DVD. However, video is highly compressed so the quality can't match MiniDV.

Camcorder formats

We like to keep boring tables to a minimum in Haynes manuals but we feel obliged to include a quick summary of the various analogue and digital recording formats. So here it is.

Format	Description	Resolution (line)*
VHS	The same size and type of video tape that your VCR uses i.e. big, bulky and relatively heavy. Most VHS camcorders are shoulder-mounted.	250
S-VHS	A souped-up, improved quality 400 version of VHS. The S is for Super.	
VHS-C	The C is for compact. A reduction in cassette size made smaller camcorders possible.	250
S-VHS-C	The benefits of S-VHS quality on a compact tape.	400
Video 8 (or 8mm)	Smaller tapes again but this format is now virtually extinct.	250
Hi-8	A higher quality version of Video 8 and the best choice for analogue camcorders.	400
Digital 8	The first of the digital formats. Digital 8 camcorders use standard Hi-8 tapes but record digital data rather than an analogue signal.	500
MiniDV	Tiny tapes, very high quality, and the norm for digital camcorders.	500+
MicroMV	A Sony format that utilises even smaller tapes and takes the digital camcorder into truly miniature realms. However, not all video editing software can capture footage from MicroMV camcorders.	500+
DVD	Yes, some camcorders record directly to small (80mm) recordable DVD discs that you can play in your PC or DVD player. But this method of recording has still to prove itself in the marketplace.	500+
Memory card	Considered more as toys than serious movie-makers, a memory card camcorder stores data on a solid-state card rather than a moving tape.	Varies

* Lines of horizontal resolution. This describes how many individual lines make up each frame of video. The more, the better, basically. However, it is only a rough guide, useful more for comparing analogue with digital formats than between different digital formats.

PART  Buying a digital camcorder

A camcorder is not a cheap purchase, and nor should it be hurried or – heaven forbid – spontaneous. But here's the thing: many buyer's guides will tell you to experiment with different models, get a feel for the controls, experiment with the optical and digital zooms, try out the image stabiliser and special effects, take a bunch away for a fortnight's intensive testing in a variety of lighting conditions, capture and compare raw footage on a computer, burn a sample DVD…

The reality, of course, is somewhat different. You're simply not going to get the chance to do any more than play with a playback button or two or flip open the odd viewfinder. The key is knowing in advance what you really need and/or want from your camcorder.

In fact, it should be possible to narrow your choice to one or two models before you set foot inside a shop. This is where review magazines and specialist websites come into their own, as you'll find ample information and informed opinion on all the latest models. But don't discount older models either, as there are often great camcorders to be picked up at a healthy discount as retailers make room for the new.

Our aim here is not to recommend any particular camcorders – our advice would be well out of date before you read it – but merely to steer you clear of the worst possible scenario, namely throwing yourself on the mercy of a commission-based superstore sales person on a busy Saturday afternoon (to whom your entreaty of 'I'm in the market for a camcorder' comes across as 'Kindly confound me with jargon for half an hour then mercilessly fleece me.').

This means understanding a little – but only a little – about digital camcorder specifications. As with any hardware, some specs are critical, some less important, and some not worth a second glance.

Take your pic! The variety of camcorders on offer is quite staggering. From left to right, we have three MiniDV devices getting progressively smaller and lighter, a tiny memory card model, a basic digital camcorder that can shoot short segments of video, and a webcam. Yes, even a humble webcam can record video footage that you can make into a movie.

Sony's MicroMV format makes it possible to make camcorders even smaller.

Format

The established MiniDV magnetic tape format is still the way to go, we reckon. Recording directly to DVD media may prove to be its successor but only if both the camcorders and blank discs are reasonably priced, and only if the technology works as well and reliably as MiniDV. There is some attraction in being able to pop a recorded DVD into a DVD player and watch your footage immediately, but you can connect virtually all digital camcorders to a television set with an analogue cable and do much the same.

Sony's MicroMV format is also appealing, particularly because the camcorders can be very small indeed. However, it's important to appreciate that video is compressed and stored in the 'lossy' MPEG-2 format at the point of shooting. This saves space on the tape but means that captured footage starts life at a lower quality level than native DV (see p25 for more on all this). Moreover, support for MicroMV camcorders is still in its infancy so your software editor may not be able to capture video from the device. One to avoid, we suggest, at least until software support can be taken for granted.

Remember, the real beauty of home movie-making is being able to edit footage on your computer to produce a professional-looking project that can be shared on DVD (or the internet). The temporary storage medium in the camcorder is far less important than what you do with that video once it's on your computer. As things stand, the universal MiniDV format works, works well, and remains the obvious choice.

Broadcast standards

An important factor but possibly not a real choice unless you buy your camcorder overseas or from a website. There are three different broadcast standards for video in the world right now: PAL, NTSC and SECAM. They are incompatible with one another, so video recorded on a PAL-format camcorder and burned to DVD will not play in an NTSC-format DVD player. In practice, though, if you live in the UK, your TV, VCR and DVD will all be PAL-compliant so all you have to do is buy a PAL camcorder to ensure compatibility.

Here's another boring table. Note that while PAL and SECAM share the same frame rate and resolution, the colour management technology is different. For full details, see **www.calfilm.com/list.htm**.

	Frame rate	Resolution	Regions
PAL	25 frames per second (interlaced), also expressed as 50Hz	625 horizontal lines	UK and most of Europe, Australia, South America
NTSC	30 frames per second (interlaced), also expressed as 60Hz	525 horizontal lines	North America, Japan
SECAM	25 frames per second (interlaced), also expressed as 50Hz	625 horizontal lines	France, Russia, Eastern Europe

A camcorder with three CCDs will generally record better video than a camcorder with just one. However, such models are still pretty pricey.

CCD

Light from the sun or a light bulb or any other source bounces off an object and hits the camcorder lens. This lens then focuses the reflected light onto an internal Charged Coupled Device (CCD). A CCD is a sensor that converts light into a digital signal that can be recorded and stored as binary data on magnetic tape. This all happens 25–30 times per second. And that's how camcorders work.

Well, more or less. A CCD is made up of a great number of pixels, usually expressed as a multiple of one megapixel (a million pixels). If a CCD has 800,000 light-sensitive pixels, you have a 0.8 megapixel camcorder; if it has 1,200,000 pixels, you have a 1.2 megapixel device. The greater the number of pixels, the better the CCD can 'see' the reflected light, and thus the higher the resolution of the final video frame.

Some camcorders go a stage further and use three CCDs. One CCD is devoted exclusively to analysing and encoding red light, one to blue light and one to green light. Such camcorders cost considerably more than single-CCD models but they are generally reckoned to produce truer, deeper, more lifelike colours and images. We wouldn't hesitate to recommend that you get a three-CCD (also known as 3-chip) camcorder if you can, but that's not to say you'll be disappointed with a single CCD.

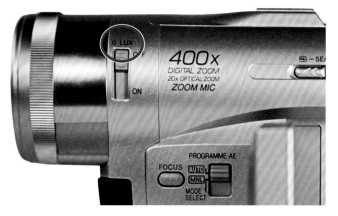

A low lux value lets you shoot at twilight or in near darkness.

Lux value

This is a measure of the camcorder's sensitivity to light. The lower the lux value, the better the camcorder can record in dim light. A cat has very low lux value eyes; you do not. A figure of 2 lux (2lx) is generally fine for twilight shoots.

Optical zoom

Being able to zoom in and out of your subject is an important and enjoyable part of filming. Most camcorders let you zoom in by a factor of 10 or more, expressed as 10x, 25x, 30x, etc. Really high optical zooms demand special, expensive lenses and are probably only warranted if you intend to film dangerous wildlife from afar, or similar.

Digital zoom

A joke, this one. Digital zoom is in reality no zoom at all. Rather, the existing image is digitally cropped and each remaining pixel then enlarged until the cropped image fills the whole frame. In this manner, it's possible to 'zoom' in on a subject by a factor of 200x or more – but it's completely worthless. You don't see any more detail. Indeed, on the contrary, digitally-zoomed video is invariably blurry, blocky and quite unwatchable. Stick with optical zoom and disable your camcorder's digital zoom feature.

Two zoom values, only one of which is worth paying any attention to.

Progressive scan

Imagine a TV screen viewed up close. What you see are lots and lots of horizontal lines. These lines are 'drawn' on a phosphorous screen coating by an electron gun firing from side to side very quickly indeed. A single frame requires a few hundred lines, and live TV demands that 25 frames (in the PAL system) or 30 frames (in the NTSC system) are drawn every second. However, while the gun draws each frame from top to bottom, it does so in two passes. On the first pass, it draws every other line and on the second pass it fills in the gaps. This is called interlacing. Virtually all TVs have interlaced displays.

There is an alternative, however, called progressive scan. Here, the lines are still drawn from side to side and from top to bottom but each line is drawn in sequence in a single pass. The result is a smoother, flicker-free, high quality picture. All computer monitors have progressive scan displays.

Now, many of the newer digital camcorders offer progressive scan recording as an alternative to interlaced recording. The difference is usually described as being more 'filmic' or 'movie-like'. However, the only way to determine whether you like the effect is to suck it and see. We will simply say here that a progressive scan option is a nice extra to have in a camcorder but is by no means essential.

On a side issue, because your monitor is a progressive scan display and your TV almost certainly isn't, you may find it worthwhile to connect a portable telly to your PC when editing footage. This will give you a better idea of how the finished movie will look on the big screen. If your computer's video card has a composite or S-Video output and your TV has a matching input, this should be easily achieved. If your TV only has SCART sockets, you can use an adapter.

Aspect ratio

Aspect ratio is the relationship between the width of an image, frame of video or display screen and its height. If you have a widescreen TV, you'll find it worthwhile shooting your footage in the 16:9 'widescreen' or 'letterbox' aspect ratio rather than the standard, squarer 4:3 ratio. This way, your movies will fill the screen without redundant black stripes either side.

However, while many camcorders now claim 16:9 support, be wary. You only get 'true' 16:9 video if the camcorder's CCD itself has a 16:9 aspect ratio. The alternative is emulated 16:9 in which a letterbox effect is overlaid on a 4:3 image. The result looks like 16:9 on a widescreen TV but frames are actually being cropped vertically and stretched horizontally to fill the screen. Resolution suffers. Definitely one to check carefully.

On the left is a true 16:9 view, in the middle is the same scene shot on a camcorder with a 4:3 aspect ratio and on the right is an emulated widescreen effect where the top and bottom of a 4:3 image are simply masked off with black bars.

Manual focus

Still something of a high-end feature, manual focus is probably a must if you're familiar with SLR cameras, and probably nothing at all to worry about if you're happy for your camcorder to focus on your subject matter automatically (something that most models manage very well indeed). If you want a manual focus, be sure to get one that works by twisting a ring on the lens, camera-style, rather than via buttons or other controls.

Digital in/out

Every digital camcorder has a FireWire output. This is what you'll use to transfer video footage to your computer. Sometimes, the FireWire socket also functions as a DV (digital video) input. The main benefit of this is that you can re-record an edited and finished movie from the computer back to the camcorder's MiniDV tape (see p137). Another, lesser, advantage is that you can capture digital video from one camcorder to another.

Re-recording from PC to camcorder tape might not be of any concern to you if you intend to turn your movies into DVDs or publish them online or archive them on a hard disk or transfer them to VHS cassettes. Moreover, a digital camcorder with a functioning digital-in socket attracts an extra tax because it is (crazily) classified in the same bracket as a video recorder. This means more expense for the manufacturer, and thus for you. Note that you can sometimes buy unsupported third-party kits that turn digital outputs into two-way sockets.

Analogue in/out

An analogue output, typically a composite video or an S-Video socket, lets you connect your camcorder to a TV set to watch raw footage directly from the tape. You can also hook it up to a VCR and save your video to VHS tape. This would be a shame, really, because you lose a good deal of the digital video's native quality in the process. However, it's a quick and convenient way of making copies, particularly for somebody who doesn't have a DVD player.

An analogue output is also desirable if your computer lacks a FireWire interface, as you can transfer your video from camcorder to computer via an analogue capture card. This again would be a pity – quality suffers – which is why we regard FireWire as an absolute must when working with digital video.

An analogue input on your camcorder is handy for capturing video from an analogue source like a VCR. If you want to make a DVD out of your wedding video, say, the most obvious route would be to connect your VCR to your PC in order to transfer the video to the hard drive with the help of recording software. This assumes that your PC has an analogue video capture card, though, and probably means lugging your VCR into the study or your PC into the living room. An easier alternative might be to connect the VCR to the camcorder's analogue input instead. Now you can copy your VHS video to the camcorder's MiniDV tape and transfer it from there to the PC later via fast FireWire.

Alternatively again, some camcorders provide an analogue-to-digital 'pass-through' mode. This sounds more complicated than it is. Basically, you connect the VCR to the camcorder's analogue input, connect the camcorder to the computer's FireWire port, and use your video capture software to import and save the video to the hard drive in real time. The video passes through the camcorder without being recorded to tape, with the camcorder

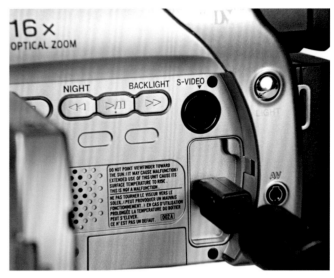

Some digital camcorders have two-way FireWire ports that function as inputs as well as outputs.

Hook up your camcorder to a TV or VCR to play your raw footage on the big screen.

rather than the computer performing the analogue-to-digital conversion (a feature sometimes expressed as ADC). This is ideal if your PC lacks an analogue video capture card or you don't want to waste time re-recording videos to the camcorder tape before getting them onto your computer.

You can use your camcorder as the middleman between an analogue video source, such as a VCR, and your computer. Either record the analogue video onto the camcorder's tape and capture it from there to the computer, or use the camcorder's ADC mode, if available, to send the video straight to the computer.

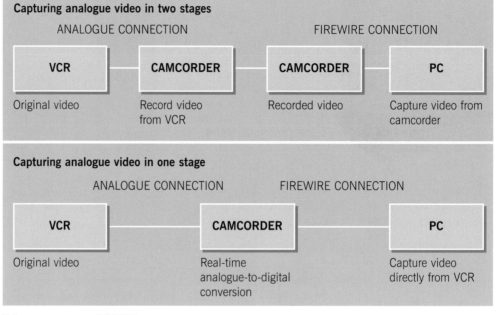

Memory card/USB

All digital camcorders can take digital still images but they store them in one of two ways: on the MiniDV tape, in which case they can only be extracted with video editing software; or on a memory card, in which case the card can be removed and read in a memory card reader. Alternatively, or additionally, many camcorders provide a USB output that allows still images to be transferred to the PC via a cable connection. The memory card itself need not then be removed.

However…the truth is that camcorders make lousy digital cameras. For the odd still snap, they're just about OK; but for anything more significant, and particularly for pictures that you want to print, invest in a dedicated digital camera.

LCD screen

Another given on MiniDV and DVD camcorders, you can use the screen to watch recorded video on the tape and as a viewfinder when shooting. The norm is a 2.5in/6.35cm diagonal screen. They deplete battery life at a rate of knots, and so are not always present in camcorders that are based on memory cards and run on standard AA or AAA batteries. Then again…

Frame your shots on the flip-out LCD screen.

Rechargeable batteries

You're likely to get one rechargeable battery in the box and you'd be well advised to purchase two or three more immediately. A single fully-charged battery should (well, may) last the duration of a one hour shoot, especially if you use the LCD screen sparingly, but what happens when you want to play the tape later? Look for a camcorder that takes either Lithium Ion or Nickel Metal Hydride batteries – avoid Nickel Cadmium – and carry charged spares at all times.

Remember to charge your batteries before you set off on a shoot.

Bolt-on accessories like special lenses and powerful microphones increase a camcorder's capabilities – and, obviously, its weight.

Control camcorder playback from across the room when it's connected to a telly.

Special features

Digital camcorders come with a bewildering array of built-in add-ons. One of the most useful is image stabilisation, which means that the camcorder attempts to compensate for slight shakiness during shooting. Results are variable but it's a nice option to have on hand, particularly if your hand is unsteady. Then again, a tripod is better still.

Night mode lets you shoot in the half-light or, if the camcorder has an infrared light, which is rare, true darkness (zero lux). Some camcorders have integrated lights for lighting close-up subjects; others have flashes for still photography; and others have attachment 'shoes' that let you bolt on more powerful spotlights. A built-in microphone is a given (as is a speaker) but look for a mic socket if you want to use a separate device.

A remote control is handy when playing back footage from the camcorder on a TV and it's very useful to be able to power the camcorder from the mains as well as by battery. One area to ignore more or less completely, however, are claims of digital special effects. For instance, a camcorder might let you shoot in black and white, or sepia, or produce negative images, or mirrored effects, or come up with 101 other tricks. But all of this should be meat for your video-editing software, not your video-shooting hardware. You'll get better results by far if you stick to shooting the best 'plain' video you can and then enhance it during the production process on your PC.

Aesthetics and more

As with portable computers, miniaturisation comes at quite a cost. A super-light, ultra-stylish camcorder is likely to lack features or cost a fortune, or both, whereas a fully-featured model may prove too heavy to carry around routinely. If there's a compromise to be struck (and when isn't there?), we suggest focusing on the key specifications first and then trying a couple of target camcorders for relative weight and 'handle' in a shop. You may find that the zoom lever on one is positioned awkwardly for your size of hand or the playback controls on another are fiddly or flimsy. Try holding an upright camcorder and compare and contrast with a low-slung model. Check where the tape compartment is located: if it's on the underside of the device, as is distressingly common, you won't be able to change tapes while the camcorder is perched on a tripod.

These are all important considerations, for you'll be using your camcorder a great deal (we hope) and it's important to get one that feels right as well as matches your performance criteria.

Wouldn't it be nice if retailers let you take camcorders on holiday just to try them out? Still, you should at least get the feel of a prospective model before splashing out. Pay particular attention to the record and zoom controls. These should be within easy reach and comfortable to use.

PART

Get your PC up to speed

There are four things you can do with camcorder footage on a computer: capture it, edit it, save it and share it. Before we consider the hardware specifications, let's just have a word or two on each of these:

Capture To capture video is to transfer a copy of it from A to B; in this case, from camcorder to computer. It's as simple as that. Moreover, because video shot on a digital camcorder is digital – i.e. binary data stored on magnetic tape – capturing it is a straightforward process of squirting data through a cable. However, you do have to use special video capturing software, as Windows alone won't do it. You will also have some choices to make during capture, such as whether you want the software to detect scene changes or to compress the video to save hard drive space. We'll explore these in Part 3.

Edit We'll be looking at video editing in great detail later but for now, if you've never tried it before, just think of words on a page. This page, for example. These words are organised in paragraphs and sections and, when read from start to finish, hopefully tell a lucid story. But that's the finished article. As I'm writing these words right now in a word processor, I can cut a sentence from here and paste it over there, shuffle paragraphs around, apply a little formatting such as **bold** or *italics*, and organise thoughts and words in any number of different ways. I can chop out sentences altogether, add words from a different document, drop in a couple of illustrative images, and so on and so forth.

Video editing works in much the same way, except that here you manipulate, shuffle and tweak video clips. For example, a

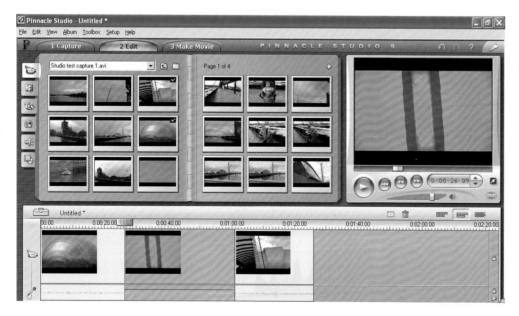

You won't be the first to mar a movie with a prolonged shot of a lens cap. But such cock-ups are easily edited out.

given clip can be trimmed for length or split into chunks that can be treated separately. You might cut and paste a clip from one point in the story to another, or intersperse your movie with still images, or rearrange the running order of consecutive scenes to tell a story backwards. You can apply special video and sound effects, link scenes with smooth transitions, add titles and captions, and much, much more. Such is the power of modern video editing software that you can often rescue seemingly duff footage.

The one thing you can't do, though, is conjure a new scene out of thin air in the way that you can write a fresh sentence or paragraph on demand. This is why it always pays to shoot more footage than you think you'll need. You never know when a second or two culled from the dullest shot will save your story.

Save When you edit video on your computer, the software keeps a record of your actions and calls it a project. You can return to a project as often as you like and complete it over several sessions. However, you don't yet have a finished movie. This requires an extra step called rendering in which your editing instructions are applied to the original video file. The end result is a finished movie in the file format of your choice. Unfortunately, the end result may take several hours to emerge because rendering is an extremely intensive computing process. You can speed it up by keeping special effects to a minimum, leaving your PC to beaver away in peace and, most importantly of all, starting off with a powerful system.

Share A finished movie stored on a computer's hard drive and watched on the monitor is, we feel, a waste. Producing a finished movie that you can play in a DVD player, post on the internet and submit to next year's Cannes Film Festival is, we suggest, a far more profitable exercise.

Specs appeal
Sad but true, not every PC on the planet is up to successful video editing. There are two potential problems: your computer may be generally underpowered, or it may lack the required hardware. Here's a summary of what you'll need.

Processor
You'll find that video editing software usually specifies at least an 800MHz processor, be it an Intel Pentium or an AMD Athlon. That's fine and dandy, you may think, but in fact it's nonsense. To work at anything like an acceptable speed, you'll need a processor running at 1.5GHz minimum and preferably faster than 2GHz. Any new-ish system will be just fine.

If you're not sure which processor you have, right-click the My Computer icon on your Desktop and select Properties from the popup menu. Click on the General tab and there you'll see a summary of your processor speed and RAM quota. A processor upgrade is not necessarily straightforward, as your computer's motherboard may not support a faster chip than the one that's currently installed. We generally recommend replacing the entire motherboard rather than upgrading a processor in isolation, as this gives you the opportunity to upgrade RAM at the same time. Speaking of which…

You can watch movies on your PC – this is Windows Media Player in one of its quirkier guises – but it's not half as satisfying as making a playable disc.

See if your PC is up to speed.

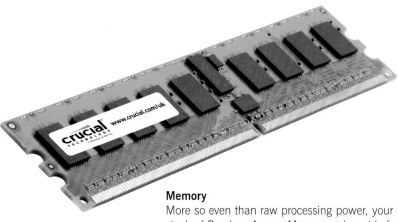

Memory

More so even than raw processing power, your PC should have a
stack of Random Access Memory onboard before tackling video
editing. Again, the software boxes will stipulate that 256MB is
required but be assured that 512MB is a realistic minimum.
Double that is better still.

Upgrading memory is easy, providing you know which modules
to buy (i.e. type, speed, capacity); you have a spare memory
slot on the motherboard; and you have the motherboard manual
to hand.

Hard drive

You'll need 13GB of free hard disk space per hour of footage
captured from your camcorder, plus a good deal more space for
storing finished movies. If you take 20GB of free space as an
absolute minimum for working with a single one-hour video, you
won't be far wrong.

It's also a good idea, although not essential, to use a separate
hard drive for capturing video. Should Windows or some
background program need access to the hard drive, there's a risk
that the flow of data will be interrupted, perhaps only for a
fraction of a second. This means that some frames may be
dropped (missed) during capture, which is obviously undesirable.

A hard drive that spins at 7,200rpm or faster is ideal but an
older 5,400rpm drive should still cope with real-time video
capture. The trick is turning off all background activity and
leaving your PC alone while it's working.

Upgrading to a larger hard drive is a cinch, particularly if you
install a second device alongside the existing drive. You won't
have to reinstall Windows or do anything else other than connect
a couple of cables and carry on working as normal. Alternatively,
simply clear off as many old files and folders as possible from
your current drive to free up some space. These could be
archived to recordable CD or DVD (see below) rather than
deleted.

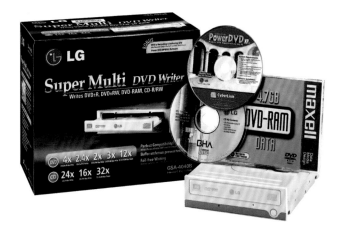

FireWire

This fast interface is an absolute must-have for capturing video from digital camcorders. Not all PCs have FireWire as standard, particularly older systems, but it's an easy upgrade. Incidentally, some sound and video cards provide a FireWire socket as a bonus so you may find that you have one even if you've never noticed or used it.

Video/sound card

The main requirement here is that your video and sound cards (or chips, if video and sound are integrated on the motherboard) should support DirectX. This is a Microsoft-developed multimedia Application Programming Interface (API) that many video editing programs use. Any reasonably recent system will be fully DirectX-compliant. Pop along to this website to update to the latest version: **www.microsoft.com/windows/directx/default.aspX**.

It's also worth updating both your video and sound card drivers to ensure that they're running at peak performance. You can look for drivers by scanning your system at the Windows update site – **http://windowsupdate.microsoft.com** – or checking the manufacturers' websites.

That aside, a 3D video card with a healthy chunk of onboard memory (ideally 32 or 64MB) will enhance your video editing and playback experience.

CD/DVD writer

If you want to make video discs that you can play in another computer or, preferably, a DVD player, you need a CD or DVD writer. This is a computer drive that can record discs as well as play them.

With a CD writer, you'll be limited to the Video CD (VCD) and Super Video CD (SVCD) formats. These discs play in most DVD players but the quality level is sub-DVD (decidedly so in the case of VCD). If you have a DVD writer, you can make bona fide DVDs that will play in virtually any DVD player.

When buying a DVD writer, be sure to get one of the multi-format models that works with DVD-R/RW and DVD+R/RW media. While your software will almost certainly work with any blank disc, your DVD player will only play it if it explicitly offers support for that recording format.

Monitor

The better your monitor, be it CRT (big, bulky) or LCD (flat, lightweight), or digital or analogue, the better your video will look. The sole real requirement is that it's big enough for you to work at a display resolution of 1024 x 768. That generally means a 17-inch CRT or a 15-inch LCD.

Windows

Not much to say here either: Windows XP handles digital video work far more successfully than any previous version and should be regarded as a pre-requisite.

Minimum requirements specified by software

These are the minimum system requirements specified by a few of the current crop of video editing programs. FireWire can be taken as read, and a CD or DVD writer as distinctly desirable.

May we just stress again that minimum really does mean minimum.

	Processor	RAM	Free hard drive space*	Version of Windows
Pinnacle Studio 9	800MHz (1.5GHz recommended)	256MB (512MB recommended)	500MB	98SE, Me, 2000, XP (XP recommended)
Ulead Video Studio 8	800MHz (2GHz recommended)	256MB (512MB recommended)	600MB (7,200rpm drive recommended)	98SE, Me, 2000, XP
Roxio Creator 7	1.2GHz	256MB	1GB	XP
Adobe Premiere Pro 1.5	800MHz (3GHz recommended)	256MB (1GB recommended)	800MB (dedicated 7,200rpm drive)	XP

* Space required for software installation alone

HARDWARE AND SOFTWARE

Software selection

Video editing software has come on immeasurably in recent years, to the extent that making movies is now both easy and rewarding. However, there is a real split between consumer products and those marketed squarely at the professional or semi-pro ('pro-sumer') videographer. 'Videographer' – what a horrible word…we promise not to use it again.

Adobe Premiere Pro is the professional's choice but far too complex – and expensive – to consider at the outset.

Top of the tree is Adobe Premiere Pro, an enormously flexible and powerful editor but one that's so far beyond the ken of beginners that it merits no discussion here. That's not a cop-out, merely a recognition that it's crazy to tackle a program as complex as Premiere Pro until you have a firm working knowledge of the basics and you feel the need to progress beyond the confines of your current software. By the end of this manual, we trust you will have achieved the former. The latter is between you and your ambition.

At the other extreme, for PC users at least, is Movie Maker 2. This is supplied as a freebie with Windows XP, presumably to rival the excellent iMovie program bundled with Macs. Movie Maker 2 is a fine way to get started but suffers from a couple of drawbacks. Most significantly, we feel, it saves videos only in a proprietary Microsoft file format called Windows Media Video (WMV). While a perfectly fine format as far as it goes, you cannot turn a finished WMV video into a playable CD or DVD without first re-encoding it as an MPEG file. Movie Maker also provides only a single soundtrack to play with – in addition to the video's own audio, that is – which complicates issues like adding narration over music or dropping in sound effects.

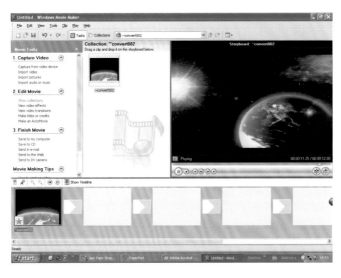

Movie Maker is free, fun and more than capable, but you'll outgrow it sooner or later.

In this book, we'll be treading the middle ground between Premiere Pro and Movie Maker. There are several programs around that offer an excellent balance between flexibility and complexity; that let you make the most of your movies without taking a degree in geekology; and that justify a relatively small outlay by producing professional-looking results that you'll be proud to showcase and share. Our two favourites are Pinnacle Studio (now in version 9) and Ulead VideoStudio (currently in version 8).

Bear in mind too that once raw footage is captured to the hard drive or simply archived on DV tape, you can return to it time and time again. It's quite possible that you'll make a simple but effective movie with Movie Maker 2 on day 1 and then rework the same footage into a Premiere Pro mini-masterpiece on day 500.

We'll be using Studio 9 throughout this manual as it offers (we think) the best balance between instant ease of use and essential features.

What to look for

Editing digital video is a popular pastime and hence we have a competitive software market out there. If you intend to be terribly thorough about the business of choosing a program, make detailed comparisons between products and pick the one that best matches your requirements. As always, though, that's easier said than done. It also begs the question of what your requirements actually are. Here is a roundup of the key features to consider.

Camcorder control

An absolute given. All digital video editors let you control the camcorder's play, rewind, fast forward, stop and other transport controls with onscreen buttons. This is just as well given that the FireWire port is usually around the back of the PC so, once connected with a cable, your camcorder may be quite out of reach.

Compression during capture

Some software offers the option of converting digital video to a compressed file format in real time during capture. For instance, the huge DV AVI video on your camcorder is saved as a much smaller MPEG-2 file on the hard drive. However – and this is a serious caveat – it takes much longer to render an edited MPEG-2 file than it does a DV AVI file. Also, the already-compressed MPEG-2 file gets put through the conversion/compression mill once again during rendering, potentially reducing the quality of video that has already been stripped of some of its native quality during capture.

Hard drive space permitting, it is always better to capture and edit footage in its original format – DV AVI – and convert it to MPEG-2 only at the final stage. If hard drive space doesn't permit, buy a new hard drive.

Incidentally, these concerns don't apply if you have a DVD or a MicroMV camcorder, because in both these cases the video is already compressed as MPEG-2 on the camcorder itself before capture. This is another reason why we prefer MiniDV.

More about file formats on p28.

There's no need to fiddle with your camcorder's controls during capture.

You can get your software to split footage into scenes during capture or when importing an existing video file, as here. Results are variable.

Credit yourself as director to round off your movie.

Scene detection

During capture, software can detect scene changes and split a video into individual scenes, or clips. This makes it very much easier to rearrange clips during editing. There are generally three methods of scene detection:

● **Reading the 'timecode' (see p33).** Whenever the software detects that recording on the camcorder was paused, it inserts a scene split.

● **Changes in content.** Notoriously flaky, this is where the software looks for significant changes in frame content between scenes. You can end up with far too many or far too few scene changes, but seldom in the appropriate places.

● **Every so often.** If you'd like to have a new scene created every ten seconds or every three minutes, no problem. But it's rather pointless.

Of course, you can create your own scenes by splitting captured video at whatever points suit you.

Preview-quality capture

Another disk space saver, this is where program captures footage from the camcorder as a highly compressed, low quality file. When you are finished editing it, the program returns to the camcorder and re-captures at full quality only those sections that made the cut. This only works if your DV tape has a continuous, unbroken timecode (see p33) and again it's not really worth the extra effort unless your hard drive is fit to burst.

Storyboard view

Individual clips are organised as graphical icons, similar to a cartoon strip.

Timeline view

Individual clips are displayed according to their respective lengths in the project as a whole. Most video editors, even Movie Maker 2, offer both storyboard and timeline views. We'll see their relative merits later.

Transitions

You can join consecutive scenes with a hard cut or a smooth transition. A transition may be a slow fade from one scene to another, a page-peeling effect or any of 1,001 alternatives.

Captions and titles

Enhance your movie with a title, rolling credits and some on-screen captions.

Special effects

Some video effects are purely for, er, effect, like slow motion, sepia colouring, picture-in-picture and strobing, while others can correct colours and rescue dim footage shot in low light.

Widescreen support

If you have a camcorder that shoots in genuine 16:9 mode rather than a cropped letterbox effect (see p16), then look for a program that captures, edits and produces video in the same format. This is becoming increasingly common.

MicroMV support

Not all video editors can (yet) capture footage from a Sony MicroMV camcorder.

Disc authoring

Many video editing programs now incorporate semi-automatic

disc 'authoring'. This is the process of burning a finished movie as a Video CD, Super Video CD or DVD disc, replete with menus. It's certainly convenient, but it's important to appreciate that standalone disc authoring tools afford a good deal more control over the structure of a project. What's vital is that your video editor can save a finished movie in the appropriate file format for a VCD, SVCD or DVD. Windows Movie Maker falls down at this juncture.

Real-time preview
When you apply a transition or a special effect, you'll naturally want to see the result before definitely committing to it in the final project. However, this requires rendering – the process by which the source footage is amended to encompass edits – and that takes time. If you have a fast computer, the software may be able to render the effect quickly enough for you to view a proper preview; if not, you will see a rough, low resolution representation of how it will look for real in the end. It can be a little hit and miss, as anybody who has waited hours to render a full project only to consider it ruined by a tacky transition or extraneous effect will confirm.

Templates, themes, styles, wizards…
Give a video editor a bunch of clips and it will stitch them together for you automatically, with or without an overall theme, titles and background music, to make a movie. Of sorts. If that appeals, read no further or skip straight to Appendix 3. But if you want full control over your output, this book is for you.

Audio support
To complement the soundtrack recorded by your camcorder, you may want to add some atmospheric background music. Virtually all video editors will work happily with MP3 and WMA files as well as WAV files (a WAV file is what you get when you copy a track from a CD). Some also support surround sound, which means you can 'upmix' a soundtrack to play on a multi-channel speaker setup, just like on a professionally-produced DVD movie. See p112-131 for more on audio.

PAL and NTSC
Most programs support both PAL and NTSC input and output (and, rarely, SECAM too) but this shouldn't be taken for granted, particularly if you buy software overseas. An NTSC-only video editor will churn out movies that you can't watch in a PAL DVD player, and vice versa.

Video file formats (ins and outs)
Any given video editor can accept a specified range of file types as source material and convert them into a specified range of output file types. At the simplest level, which may in fact be all you ever need to worry about, the program captures video from the camcorder in its native high resolution format (DV AVI) and converts it to one of the MPEG file formats after editing in readiness for burning a VCD, SVCD or DVD.

Beyond this, video editors can usually accept other file types as input material, such as video clips downloaded from the internet. Moreover, they can output videos in other formats than MPEG-1 and 2. If you want to publish a video on your website, for instance, you'd probably want to select a highly compressed file format.

The wider a program's file support, the more useful you will find it if you work regularly with different types of digital video.

From hard drive to DVD in simple steps.

Be sure that your software makes movies that match your DVD player and TV broadcast standard. Virtually all editors handle both PAL and NTSC.

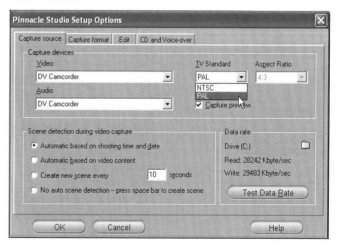

Format	Description	Typical use
DV AVI (Digital Video Audio Video Interleaved)	AVI is a codec used to compress video. On a digital camcorder's MiniDV tape, footage is stored in this format (sometimes also called DV25).	Capturing video from a camcorder without applying any further compression or conversion process
MPEG-1 (Motion Picture Experts Group Format 1)	Heavily compresses AVI files, with the emphasis on small file sizes.	Making VCDs
MPEG-2 (Motion Picture Experts Group Format 2)	A more flexible upgrade to MPEG-1 with smarter compression technology. The focus here is on quality at the expense of small file sizes.	Making SVCDs Making DVDs Recording format used by MicroMV and DVD camcorders
MPEG-4 (Motion Picture Experts Group Format 4)	The latest addition to the MPEG 'brand', based on the QuickTime format, this offers very small file sizes while maintaining high video quality.	Internet video Recording format for camcorders based on memory cards
QuickTime	Primarily an Apple file format, QuickTime files usually have an MOV extension. To view a QuickTime file, you need the free QuickTime Player program (**www.quicktime.com**).	Internet video
WMV (Windows Media Video)	A very efficient compression format, similar to MPEG-1 and MPEG-2, depending on its settings. The WMV format is not compatible with the VCD, SVCD or DVD formats.	Internet video Movie Maker videos
RealVideo	A rival to QuickTime and WMV formats. To watch a RealVideo file, you need the free RealPlayer program (**www.real.com**).	Internet video
ASF (Active Streaming Format)	An older Microsoft format, now superseded by WMV. One to forget.	Internet video
DivX	Based on MPEG-4 codec, and arguably superior, DivX produces very high quality video with small file sizes.	Internet video Squeezing high quality movies onto CD or DVD Potentially an alternative to DVD (some DVD players now support DivX discs)

Too high a degree of compression leads very quickly to blockiness or blurriness. Striking a balance between video quality and file size is the key.

Video file formats explored

The table above is a summary of the current crop of digital video file formats. Be warned, it will make your head spin. The thing to remember is that any format is essentially an attempt to preserve the greatest possible video quality with the smallest possible file size.

The case for compression

In an ideal world, all digital video would be enjoyed at the best possible quality level, all the time. But in the real world, compromises must be made. Before recordable DVD drives became available and affordable, the only way to enjoy a home movie on a DVD player was to burn it to CD. This meant significantly reducing the quality level to squeeze footage onto the disc (i.e. the VCD format), or maintaining the quality but sacrificing playback time (i.e. the SVCD format). When you have a 4.7GB recordable DVD to play with, it's possible to have high quality and long playback. However, compression still plays an important part: to fit an hour of digital video on a disc means squeezing the original 13GB DV AVI file down to about a third of its original size. That's where you'd use the MPEG-2 codec.

On the internet, the problem of distributing video is even more acute. Viewers have to download millions of bits and bytes through their modems before they can see a video, and a low resolution clip that downloads in a couple of minutes (a 1MB file, say) will be more welcome than the same clip at a higher resolution if it takes an hour to appear.

The mechanics of compression is complex to the point of mind-numbing tedium but the goal and principle are easy enough to grasp. The goal is to reduce a given file size to X dimensions while preserving quality level Y. Both X and Y are variables dictated by the task at hand. If you want to fit 30 minutes of video onto a single CD, you'll need to produce a final file size of around 650MB; and if you know you have 650MB to play with, you'll want to compress the video until it just fits and no more. Quite what counts as acceptable playback quality is open to subjective interpretation, of course. Some long-term DVD aficionados consider VCDs an affront to all that's decent in the digital world, while a newcomer watching a stop–start stamp-sized video on a website might well be amazed that such things are possible at all.

A codec moment

The way to reduce a file size is to compress it, which means throwing out much of the data that makes up the original video. Not just any data, mind, but data that we don't need. For instance, in any given scene, chances are the background remains more or less static while the subject struts its stuff. In the original footage shot on your camcorder, the background is captured and encoded by the CCD 25 times every second. That requires an awful lot of data to record the same thing over and over again. What compression does is strip out such redundancy by remembering the background details from one frame and encoding changes between frames only when necessary. In a compressed video, an unchanging background requires only one full frame's worth of data – a so-called 'key frame' – plus a lot of smaller backward references in subsequent frames. When the background does change, the original key frame is abandoned and the current frame becomes the new benchmark. Succeeding frames are then compared to the new key frame, and only changes are recorded…and so on.

This is why, incidentally, it's unwise to import in the MPEG format. Every frame in an MPEG video contains information only about the changes since the last key frame, so applying an edit, effect or transition forces the software to cross-reference preceding frames. This takes a great deal of time and the result can be disappointing. In a DV AVI file, however, every frame is effectively self-contained.

Other blunter compression techniques include reducing the frame size (smaller frames require less data), frame rate (fewer frames require less data), and reducing the number of colours that are displayed. Audio quality can also be sacrificed in the pursuit of smaller files.

Compression is handled by a codec, a term derived from compression/decompression. The best codecs offer a range of options that allow you to tailor a video to the project at hand. We'll see codecs in practice when we come to saving and producing a finished movie (see p138).

For now, just bear in mind one potential problem with codecs. When you try to play a video file on your computer, it will only work if the computer has the same codec installed on it as was used to encode the file. In the case of QuickTime and RealVideo files, you also have to download a separate (free) software player.

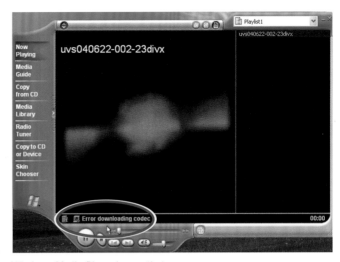

Windows Media Player knows that it needs a specific codec to play the video – but fails to find it.

This is, basically, a drag. If you download a DivX video from the internet, for example, you can only watch it if you first download and install the DivX codec on your PC. Windows Media Player usually downloads codecs automatically on an ad hoc basis but it won't fetch DivX for you. In fact, Windows Media Player can't even play MPEG-2 videos (or DVD movies) unless you have an MPEG-2 codec installed somewhere on your system. This would usually be provided by a third-party DVD player program, like PowerDVD.

But we digress. In the end, codecs, compression and file formats all boil down to getting the best possible video to match a given set of circumstances. If your primary goal is making movies with your digital camcorder and sharing them on CD or DVD, the conversion equation remains simple: DV AVI direct from your camcorder tape as the input and MPEG-2 as the output.

The first time you try to play a QuickTime video (file extension MOV) in Windows Media Player, it offers this less than helpful dialogue. What you need is the QuickTime Player.

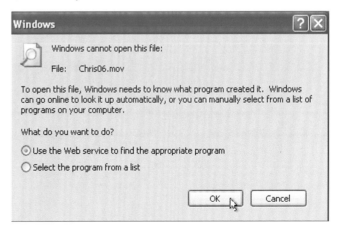

PART **2** DIGITAL VIDEO MANUAL
Successful shooting

PART 2 Preparation

The first secret of shooting decent footage is being properly prepared. Now we're not going to make a big deal out of this; after all, the intrinsic appeal of owning a digital camcorder is that you can take it anywhere and start shooting at a moment's notice. All the same, much frustration can be avoided if your kit is in a state of readiness come that moment.

This is a big, bolt-on, no-brand 'compatible' battery that lasts considerably longer than the battery originally supplied with the camcorder. Be sure that any such battery you buy is correctly rated for your camcorder.

What you need to take

We'll assume here that you own a digital camcorder. We'll also assume that you are relatively new to the video game rather than a seasoned pro. Here's a pre-shoot checklist.

Batteries

If you work on the optimistic basis that one fully-charged battery will last for an hour's shoot, have a guess how long you'll be filming and plan accordingly. Better still, carry three or four batteries with you at all times. They are very expensive but they do last a long time. Incidentally, your camcorder will probably be supplied with the lowest spec battery from the range. An alternative battery with a higher milliamp hour (mAh) rating may be larger and heavier and take longer to charge, but it will also run for considerably longer. For safety's sake, you're better off buying the manufacturer's own batteries. An alternative brand of battery, even if you find one that fits, may operate at a different voltage and could damage the camcorder.

You can't have too many spare batteries.

Tapes

A real no-brainer: stock up on blank MiniDV tapes and take more than enough with you. They are cheaper to buy in bulk, even five at a time, than singly. Free them from their shrink-wrapped cellophane and label each with one of the sticky labels supplied. This will make it easier to scrawl a note of the tape's contents as you fill them up (obvious but essential: we have a box of foolishly unlabelled MiniDV tapes that proves the point).

Also consider 'striping' your tapes. This is the decidedly odd business of inserting a new tape in the camcorder and recording nothing at all from start to finish in one unbroken session with the lens cap on. The point of striping is that it records an unbroken timecode throughout the entire tape. This is important when it comes to automatic scene detection during capture (see p26) and if you want to capture footage at preview quality (see p26). But why?

The issue is that during an average shoot, you will stop and start recording many times. Let's call each recording a scene. When you first begin recording on a new tape, the timecode starts from zero (00.00.00). So long as each successive scene follows on from where the last scene ends, the timecode will run smoothly from start to finish. For instance, your first scene might take you from 00.00.00 to 00.02.30, and your second scene from 00.02.31 to 00.05.45. However, it's likely that you'll want to review your footage as you go long – one of the beauties of digital video is instant replay – and the chances of you stopping the tape during playback at precisely the point where the last scene finishes are remote. It's far more probable that you'll overrun the end of the previous scene by a second or two.

And that's the problem: there is now a gap in the timecode, the camcorder is liable to start recording from 00.00.00 all over again, and your capture software won't be able to detect scenes by reference to the timecode. Striping solves this by 'formatting' the tape with a timecode before you begin shooting for real.

If you do decide to stripe tapes, keep the camcorder connected to the mains power to save its batteries. If you can't be bothered – and who can blame you? – there are four alternatives.

- First, forget all about automatic scene capture or preview capture and do your own scene-splitting once the entire tape has been captured onto your computer.
- Secondly, don't review your footage as you go along: just stop and start recording every time.
- Thirdly, if you do review footage, be sure to overlap each new scene with the end of the last one. It means losing a few frames from the end of the scene but it does preserve the timecode.
- Finally, your camcorder itself may have a 'seek end' or 'blank search' or similar function that automatically finds the final frame of the last recorded scene and cues up the tape in precisely the right spot for the next shoot. This too preserves a perfect timecode.

A little labelling goes a long way.

With the lens cap on and the camcorder powered from the mains, record all the way through your new tapes to imprint a continuous timecode.

OK, so this isn't exactly your professional-level tripod, but anything that aids stability is a blessing.

Tripod

If there's one accessory that we can guarantee will dramatically improve your raw footage, it's a half-decent tripod. This will let you shoot perfectly level, pan slowly and smoothly, zoom without the wobbles, and eliminate that familiar hand-shake that mars so many home movies. Yes, you have to lug the thing around with you, but we strongly suggest you do just that whenever possible.

Tripods comes in a bewildering array of shapes and sizes, with prices to match. The key specs, though, are straightforward:

- **Fluid head.** This guarantees that your pans will be smooth, not jerky.
- **Quick release head.** When you need to change the tape or want to whisk your camcorder away for a spot of handheld action, the last thing you need is a five minute tussle with your tripod. A quick release head frees the camcorder instantly.
- **Adjustable tension.** You control a tripod-mounted camcorder with a boom. This should have a twist handle that slackens or tightens the tension. When shooting a straight shot, you should be able to tighten it fully to keep the camcorder perfectly steady; and when panning, you should be able to loosen it to just the right degree of resistance to sweep from side to side smoothly.
- **Lightweight but sturdy.** A tripod should be strong enough to stand up straight in a breeze but light enough to be humped from A to B without breaking your back or your resolve.
- **Spirit level.** An integrated spirit level is handy for ensuring that you're shooting perfectly straight. However, you can always use the horizon as a guide when shooting outdoors, or a window or door frame when inside. Or just your own sense of what looks right.

A fluid head tripod with an adjustable boom.

This camcorder has sockets for both headphones and an external microphone.

Microphone and headphones

We'd have to classify these both as optional extras rather than essentials. The point of an external microphone is clear – better sound quality. You can get closer to a subject without sticking the camcorder in their face and there is a reduced risk of picking up your own coughs and sneezes or the sound of the camcorder's tape mechanism. But not all camcorders have a microphone jack and not all have somewhere to bolt a microphone on. A handheld mic is a possibility but only if you have a sound assistant.

Headphones may seem unimportant but in fact they give you a very clear indication of what sounds the camcorder is recording rather than just what you hear with your own ears. Your camcorder's headphone socket, if it has one, probably doubles-up as the analogue output.

Bag

Just a padded camera bag to carry everything in. Don't forget to pack a pen (for labelling tapes); an analogue cable (S-Video or composite video, plus a SCART adapter) to connect the camcorder to a TV for playback, should the opportunity present itself; a USB cable if you'll want to transfer still images from the camcorder's memory card to a computer; and perhaps also a FireWire cable if you'll be needing to transfer footage to a PC before you return to base.

And the remote control.

And a spare lens cap.

And your battery charger lest you get the chance/have the need to recharge batteries mid-shoot.

And the camcorder's wrist strap and shoulder strap.

Best make it a big bag.

What you need to know

You need to know how to operate your camcorder, in a nutshell, and for that you need the camcorder manual. If, like us, a manual is the last thing you want to read (except this one), then these are the essential areas to familiarise yourself with.

Tape compartment

A MiniDV tape is installed inside the body of a camcorder, and this usually means working with a motorised but awkward tape-loading mechanism. Don't be surprised to find a 'Don't Press Here!' sticker somewhere on precisely the part of the tape compartment cover that you instinctively want to press. Equally, don't be surprised if you break the camcorder by ignoring this warning.

In our experience, no two camcorders from different manufacturers have quite the same tape compartment design. Here we show how to load a fresh tape on a Canon model.

The tape compartment cover is located on the base of the camcorder. This is not unusual but it does mean that you have to remove the device from a tripod before you can swap tapes. Anyway, the first stage is simply flipping open a manual cover. You'll need to have the camcorder connected to the mains or powered by a battery at this point, as opening the cover activates the motorised mechanism. Note that ominous warning sticker.

❷

Depending on the design, the tape-holding section of the tape compartment should now emerge partially from the compartment. Pop in a tape. It will only fit one way, and you must avoid applying any force. Now consult the manual, check the stickers, or both and determine just how to close the compartment door safely. In this case, which is pretty standard, the trick is pressing down very lightly on the top of the protruding tape holder.

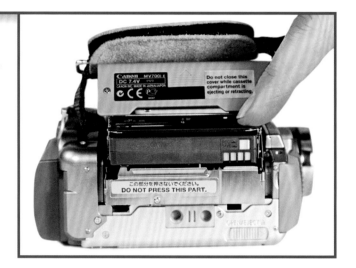

❸

This action prompts the camcorder to suck the tape into the tape compartment. Note that no force has been applied, just the gentlest pressure. When the tape is safely inside, you can close the manual tape compartment cover.

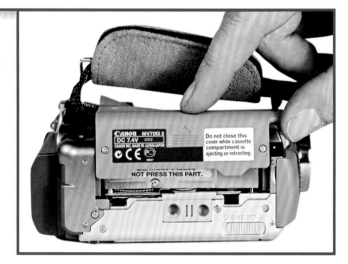

❹

Loaded and ready to shoot. For all this is a fiddly procedure, it does hammer home the clever design of these devices.

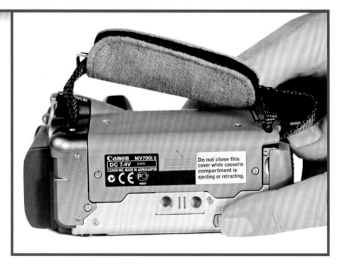

Camera/VCR mode

Your camcorder will have a switch that toggles between recording and playback modes, often labelled camera and VCR. A big red (usually) button will activate recording.

Zoom lever

This is usually a finger-operated slider or lever that controls the camcorder's optical and, if present, digital zoom functions. You may find that the digital zoom function is disabled by default, which is just as it should be.

LCD screen/viewfinder

You have two ways to monitor video recording and playback: a viewfinder, which may or may not be adjustable, and an LCD screen, which should certainly flip and probably rotates through 180 degrees. The benefit of rotation is that you can point the camcorder at yourself for a self-portrait or talking head shot and see how it will look. Always bear in mind that the LCD screen draws heavily on battery power. However, many people prefer to frame shots with the screen rather than the viewfinder, in which case spare batteries are, as ever, sensible.

Zoom control

LCD screen

On/off/mode/record button

Transport controls

Just like a VCR – which is, of course, what it is – your camcorder will have 'transport' controls with which to control playback of the MiniDV tape. Typically you'll have play, rewind, fast forward, pause and stop buttons. To watch some recently recorded footage, you switch the camcorder to VCR mode, rewind the tape and press Play.

Auto/manual focus

Camcorders are very adept at focusing on the subject, particularly if that subject is centre-frame. If you'd prefer to focus on, for instance, a background character in order to intentionally blur a foreground subject, turn to your camcorder's manual focus feature (if present). As mentioned on p17, a twisting ring on the lens is easy to work with while a manual focus controlled with buttons is generally a pain.

Transport controls

Focus and exposure controls

Auto/manual exposure

Camcorders automatically adjust to the available light, which is probably what you want in most circumstances. If, however, you pan from a brightly-lit scene to a dimly-lit scene, such as when shooting through a window at a sunny outside world and then panning back into the room, it takes a moment or two for the camcorder to adjust. This is reflected in recorded footage by a few seconds of rapid fluctuation in the light level as the camcorder struggles to find the right balance. However, if your camcorder has a manual exposure feature, you can adjust the exposure to suit one scene or the other and then lock it in place. This prevents fluctuations in light levels.

Light

Some camcorders have their own built-in 'key' or 'assist' lights with which to illuminate a relatively close subject. As you can imagine, such lights drain batteries like pulling the plug in a bath. In our experience, they also tend more to highlight shiny noses than to do a human subject any favours.

A key light can be handy but it's no substitute for a proper lighting rig.

White balance

As any photographer knows, light has a 'temperature'. The cooler the temperature, the redder the overall appearance of a scene; the warmer the temperature, the bluer everything appears. Camcorders know this and adjust their white balance according to how they 'see' the current light. The principle is that white is a constant baseline to which the camcorder can refer in order to adjust its interpretation of other colours. This way, a green jumper will look (roughly) the same shade of green when videoed in sunshine or under a lightbulb. If you've ever noticed the colours in a video changing without apparent reason when you cut or pan from one room to another, this is the camcorder's automatic white balance in action.

Here again you can give your camcorder a helping hand. Point the camcorder at something pure white, like a sheet of paper (a cream, grey or magnolia wall is no use), then zoom in until it fills the entire screen and flick the switch, push the button, activate the on-screen display function, or whatever you have to do to lock the white balance at the current setting. You colours should now appear more natural. Repeat as often as required, which means whenever your lighting changes significantly.

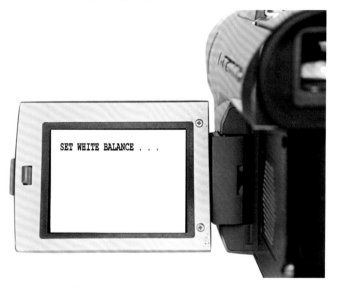

The easiest way to ensure faithful colour reproduction is to show your camcorder what true white looks like under the current lighting conditions.

Standard play/long play

Most camcorders can stretch a 60 minute tape into 90 minutes. But doing so degrades the quality of the footage, so don't do it unless you have no choice e.g. you're heading towards the end of your last tape and the action is unmissable.

On-screen display (OSD)

Many of your camcorder's functions will be accessed and managed by means of menus on an OSD, including the likes of image stabilisation and 'end search' features. There is no standard as such for these menus, so work through your camcorder manual.

SUCCESSFUL SHOOTING

The shoot

We're simply not able to tell you how to shoot superb video footage in a couple of pages. That would require its very own manual and we'd have no space for the fun stuff like editing captured video and producing DVDs. All we can really do here is point out a couple of common mistakes and make a few positive suggestions. The rest is between you, your camcorder and your creativity.

Planning

When film directors shoot a scene, they generally have the benefit of rehearsals, obedient actors and a script. You, however, are unlikely to have anything like the same level of control over what you shoot. Indeed, you may have no control whatsoever: try asking a bride-to-be to pause for a close-up while en route up the aisle and you'll see what we mean. When it rains, it rains; and when your subject happens to be between you and the glaring sun, it's tough.

   If nothing else, though, you can think about positioning. Whatever your subject matter, be it a birthday party, a sporting event, a landscape or children splashing in a paddling pool, try to imagine how it would look best shown on a television or in a film. Then get yourself in the position to shoot accordingly. If you want to learn how to shoot a wedding scene, crib from *The Godfather*; to see how not to shoot a tedious school play, sit through a performance of any proud parent's single-angle home video.

When looking for the best filming position, take a tip from the experts. If you see a professional photographer set up his stall, sidle in and shoot some footage from the same perspective.

Structure

Odd-sounding advice, perhaps, but we recommend that you don't worry too much about movie-making itself during a shoot and concentrate instead on filming anything and everything that comes to mind or into view. Let your imagination run riot unrestricted by logic or order or thoughts of telling a story. Don't even bother reviewing your footage as you go along except to check angles and lighting. The point is that you'll have ample opportunity to assemble and edit your footage later; and the more you have to work with, the better. We guarantee that you'll be grateful for those unplanned scenes and spur of the moment snaps when you get to the editing suite.

Lighting

Good lighting is the key to good footage. Unfortunately, good lighting comes at a considerable cost and inconvenience. If you're up for carting arc lamps and spotlights around, and if your subjects are prepared or able to hang around while you compose the perfectly lit shot, good luck. But most of us have to make do with the lighting on hand, be it natural or artificial.

A handful of tips:

- Adjust your camcorder's white balance manually as described above. This gives you the best possible chance of capturing lifelike colours and tones whether you're shooting on a sunny beach or at dusk or under a stark fluorescent strip-light.
- Avoid backlit subjects if at all possible. A backlit subject is one where the subject is situated between you and the main light source. A classic example would be somebody sitting in front of a window or standing with the sun at their back. In such cases, the camcorder adjusts its exposure to compensate for the flood of light and your subject gets cast into semi-darkness. While a gently backlit scene has extra depth, it's a tricky balance to get right so, if you can, keep the light behind the camcorder.

Of course, this advice is largely theoretical: when the sun's coming up behind your mountain subject, the only way to avoid backlighting may be to turn the camera through 180 degrees, which rather misses the point (and the mountain). Still, if your camcorder has a backlight compensator, give it a try. This should lighten foreground backlit subjects to a degree. You can also try lighting a foreground subject with an additional light source. This works better with close-up people than distant mountains.

- Don't shoot the sun. Although pointing your camcorder directly at the heavens can generate some lovely video effects, it can also permanently damage the camcorder's CCD.
- If you do have access to additional light sources, the three areas to focus on are key lighting (lighting your subject, often involving the use of reflectors or filters for a soft, natural look); fill lighting (selectively lighting other areas of your scene, usually to avoid conspicuous shadows or for effect); and background lighting (lighting the background to add depth to the shot).

You can achieve surprisingly good or different effects simply by playing around with any light source you have to hand – try redirecting an angle-poise lamp – but setting up a professional lighting rig is a skilled task beyond the scope of this book.

The classic mistake of shooting a subject with the main light source behind them.

Pretty, but dangerous.

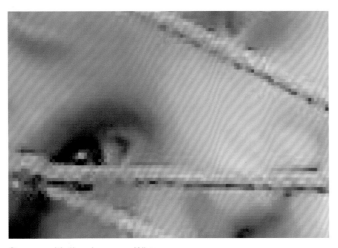

Go easy with the close-ups. When you push a digital zoom to the max, pixelation soon sets in.

Panning and zooming

The truth is that it's tempting to pan and zoom at every opportunity. But while the odd side-sweep or close-up is certainly a valid part of most projects, excessive use of these effects is a big mistake. Pans are basically boring, particularly when a holiday video consists of endless broad landscape shots. Unless you're using a tripod, your pans are also liable to be shaky and jerky, especially if you use zoom at the same time. We also tend to pan too quickly, particularly when shooting action. This is headache-inducing at best and, on an interlaced camcorder, can cause frames to break up. When you zoom in or out on a subject, do so slowly and steadily.

Sound

When you use the camcorder's internal microphone, it focuses on the direction in which the camcorder is pointing. Again, we suggest that you use headphones where possible to hear what the camcorder hears. Shelter the mic grill from wind noise (your camcorder may have a noise-reduction feature that can help here) and try to avoid sneezing while shooting. Also be sure to use your camcorder's highest audio recording setting, typically 16-bit.

If you find that your camcorder picks up the sound of its own motorised tape compartment – something that should be unforgivable but is in fact not uncommon – it's worth investing in a separate bolt-on or handheld mic.

In fact, the importance of audio is often underestimated in movies, particularly the home-grown variety. While the odd shaky camera shot can add a certain amateur appeal, an indistinct, muffled or wind-blown soundtrack simply sounds duff and puts viewers off.

An add-on directional microphone can help enormously but the serious film maker will need to invoke a sound assistant to hold a boom mic or set up each shot in such a way that the audio is picked up precisely, or both. Like lighting, your videos will turn out all the better for this upfront effort; but like lighting, it supposes that you have the wherewithal – time, money, inclination, expertise – to set up each scene. For most of us, most of the time, shooting video with a digital camcorder is a case of picking up the camera and shooting from the hip (or shoulder), not an exercise in studio production.

Besides, you'll find that you can enhance or even mask the original soundtrack with atmospheric background music, narration and sound effects later on.

Framing and composition

Give 9 out of 10 of us a camcorder and a subject to shoot, and we'll put that subject squarely in the centre of the frame. But if you spend a little time watching TV programmes or films, you'll notice that central framing is actually rather rare. Moreover, there's usually a balance to be struck between zooming in too closely on a subject and showing too much of the background. And then you have the choice of shooting straight-on or slightly from an angle, or shooting level or from above or from below, and so forth…

Framing a shot is something you'll learn on the job, or more likely later on when you come to edit your footage. There are 'rules' of a sort but a little self-criticism and experimentation are more profitable than slavish acceptance of the norm. Next time

Shoot from a child's perspective to see the world through different eyes.

you find yourself watching an uninteresting scene in your video editing program, ask yourself how you could have shot that scene better.

Here are the customary top tips:

- Shoot children at their own level. Footage of a party or kids at play is much more engrossing when viewed from their perspective rather than your own.
- If a human subject is looking off to the left, position them to the right of the frame to leave some 'lead space' in the shot.
- Similarly, when filming a subject that's moving from left to right, keep it to the left of the frame rather than central. Otherwise it looks like the subject will run into the edge of the frame, which is disconcerting for the viewer (try it and see).
- Don't zoom in too closely on people: always leave a little free space above their heads – but not too much – and avoid chopping them off at the knee.
- Tempting though it is to keep the camcorder static on a tripod or clutched to your eye, try shooting on the hoof. This is particularly effective when filming a moving subject. The twofold trick, of course, is keeping the camera steady and not tripping up as you walk. Get a friend to push you around in a trolley or on a skateboard, or just practice, practice, practice. Your camcorder's image stabilisation feature will prove helpful here but it can't cope with excessive camera shake.
- Always keep one eye and ear on the background. A blaring telly in another room will compete for the viewer's aural attention with baby's first gurgles.
- Finally, and most importantly, observe the 'rule of thirds'. The most famous guide to shot composition is to mentally divide the frame into nine segments formed from two horizontal and two vertical imaginary lines. Now position your main subject roughly at one of the four intersection points. Your movies will look 'right' – and just like everybody else's.

There's a lot to be said for the rule of thirds, and it certainly provides a useful and easy point of reference when framing a shot. When shooting a landscape, for instance, position the horizon one third up from the bottom of the frame or one third down from the top rather than in the middle. When filming a face, frame it so that the eyes – which are the most important element in the shot – are similarly positioned. If there's a mountain in the distance, frame it one third in from either side.

Focus

Starting a shot out of focus and gradually bringing the subject into focus is an effective filming technique, albeit tiresome if used excessively. If your camcorder has a manual focus, give it a try. It is, however, essential to keep the camcorder absolutely steady while focusing. Also bear in mind that you can add a fade-in focus effect in your video editor later.

Digital effects

Once again, let us stress that you should forget about your camcorder's built-in effects during a shoot. Sure, it may offer a sepia-tinted filter or a mosaic option that transforms any scene into a kaleidoscopic riot of colour – but so what? Your video editing software will do this too, and do it better. Keep your source footage 'clean'. Remember, if you apply an effect with the camcorder during the shoot, you're stuck with it forever, whereas with your software you can experiment and take the time to get it right.

Four imaginary lines with four intersections: the bluffer's guide to perfect composition.

Give your subjects some lead space to avoid collisions with the edge of the frame.

Your camcorder may come equipped with a bunch of digital effects but we'd advise you to give them a wide berth.

3

PART 3 Capturing video from camcorder to computer

PART

Preparation

Capturing video is the business of transferring or copying footage from the tape in your digital camcorder to the computer's hard disk. Once captured, your footage can be edited and made into a movie.

Video capture through FireWire is a real-time process, which means that one hour of footage takes one hour to capture. Barring accidents, you'll end up with a perfect copy of your source footage.

Capturing video is easy. In fact, it's boring. However, given that one hour of digital video requires approximately 13GB of free disk space and given that both the hard disk and your computer should be optimised for video capture before you begin, let's pause for a quick glance at the hardware.

Tweak your hard disk

Tend to your hard disk up front and it will, or should, reward you with a perfect capture every time. Specifically, you should avoid the bane of dropped frames where, for whatever reason, the drive doesn't keep pace with the flow of data through the FireWire port.

Check disk space

To see how much free disk space you have currently, double-click the My Computer icon on your Desktop (or open My Computer from the Start menu) and right-click the hard drive icon. From the popup menu, select Properties. The General tab now displays the disk as a two-coloured pie where blue represents used space and pink represents free space. As a guide, you should have 50% free space over and above what you need for capture alone to allow for editing. So, if you intend to capture and edit one hour of footage, you should have around 20GB of free space. More can't hurt. Now is the time to archive or even delete older files to free up disk space.

Although relatively large, this 80GB hard drive is already close to capacity.

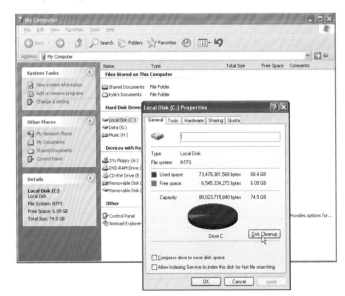

Defragment the disk

Over time, files stored on the hard disk get split into separate parts and stored piecemeal over the platters that form the physical surface of the disk. This process is known as fragmentation. While Windows can always (well, almost always) retrieve a fragmented file, it takes longer to patch together than an unfragmented file. The worse the degree of file fragmentation, the harder the hard disk has to work. This makes no discernible difference with small, everyday files, but it can have an impact with gargantuan video files.

When capturing digital video, it helps to defragment the hard disk at the outset. This rebuilds existing files and sets aside a contiguous, unbroken slice of hard disk space in readiness for new files. The upshot is that the captured video can be saved without fragmentation and thereafter accessed without delays.

To defragment your hard disk, use the Windows utility called, unsurprisingly, Disk Defragmenter. Click Start > Programs > Accessories > System Tools > Disk Defragmenter. Select (highlight) your target hard disk in the upper window – C: drive, usually – and click the Defragment button. Then leave the computer alone for an hour or two.

Use the Analyze button to determine whether your hard disk desperately needs defragmenting – or just go for it anyway.

Enable DMA

Direct Memory Access (DMA) is a setting that allows a drive to send data to and from system memory, or RAM, without going through the processor first. This direct route helps to avoid dropped frames. To check the setting if you're running Windows 98 or Millennium Edition, click Start > Settings > Control Panel and double-click the System icon. Now open the Device Manager tab and expand the Disk drives section. Right-click the icon that represents your hard disk, select Properties from the popup menu and open the Settings tab. Finally, put a check mark in the DMA box (unless there's one there already). Repeat for any other hard disks in your system.

In Windows XP, DMA is turned on by default so no changes are required.

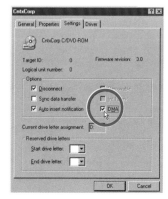

Direct Memory Access is essential for capturing video smoothly.

When frames are dropped during capture, chances are your computer is busy elsewhere. Allow it to focus completely on the task in hand.

Frippery-free

Before commencing a capture procedure, turn off any screen savers, close down all programs other than your video capture software, and ensure that no scheduled tasks are liable to cut in. A routine anti-virus sweep that kicks in mid-capture could prove disastrous. In fact, consider switching off your anti-virus program altogether to stop it needlessly scanning the newly created video file. Finally, be warned that any attempt to multi-task during video capture – i.e. doing anything at all with your computer other than watching the screen – is liable to interrupt disk writing and, again, cause frames to be dropped.

A dedicated disk?

While you can capture digital video directly to the same hard disk that's running Windows and hosts all your other software, files and folders, it's preferable to use a separate disk altogether. This can be a second hard disk installed alongside the primary disk, or an external model connected via FireWire or USB 2 (but not the older, slower USB 1.1 standard). It can even be a disk partition, which is to say a fixed area of a hard disk constituted to behave like a physically distinct device.

You'll need a third-party program to partition a hard disk, such as Partition Magic from Symantec (**www.symantec.com**). But with hard disks now so cheap, why not simply slot in a spare and save yourself the trouble?

NTFS or bust

Hard disks can be formatted in one of two ways: FAT32, commonly used for Windows 98 and Me, and NTFS, used for Windows 2000 and XP. Unfortunately, FAT32 disks can't handle

A partitioned hard disk is a good second-best alternative to a spare disk devoted to capturing and storing video.

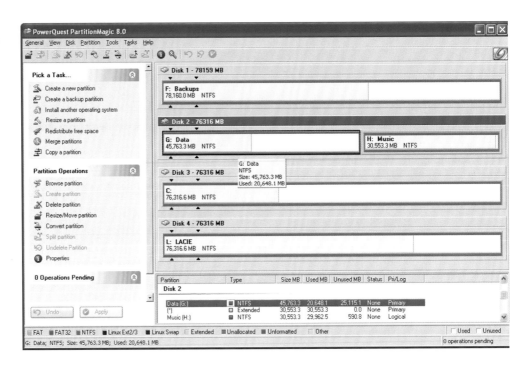

file sizes greater than 4GB, so you won't be able to capture more than around 20 minutes of video at a time. That's not a complete disaster, for you can still edit clips from different capture sessions into a finished movie and save it as a sub-4GB file. However, NTFS has no such file size restrictions and is clearly the way to go with digital video.

To check your current configuration in Windows XP, open the My Computer folder, right-click your hard disk, and select Properties. In the General tab, look for the File system entry. If it says FAT32, chances are you (or somebody) upgraded this PC to Windows XP and declined to change the file system at the same time. No matter: you can upgrade to NTFS now.

- Click Start
- Click Run
- Type 'cmd' (without the quotes)
- Click OK.
- Type 'convert c: /fs:ntfs' (again without the quotes, and noting the space after the colon).

If you are formatting a different drive, replace c: with the appropriate drive letter, such as d: or e:. If it all sounds a touch daunting, see the following help page from Microsoft's Knowledge Base: **http://support.microsoft.com/default.aspX?scid=kb;en-us;307881**.

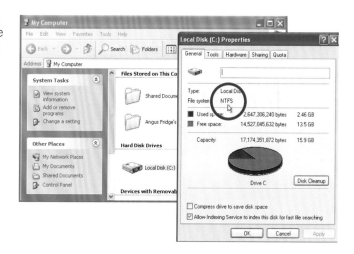

NTFS is the file system of choice.

Install – and patch – your software

You can't capture video from a digital camcorder with Windows alone so it's time to install your video editor. In the following guides, we'll be working mainly with Pinnacle Studio version 9 and a little bit with Ulead VideoStudio version 8. You may use a different program altogether, of course, but the basic methodology will be the same.

Install your program and, if required, register or 'activate' it online. We've come to learn that one of the characteristics of video editing software is a need for frequent updates. Sometimes, an update adds a new feature that wasn't available when the CD was pressed, like support for extra file formats or CD/DVD writers; and sometimes it merely fixes a program that was rushed to market rather too early or has undergone insufficient field trials. When we first installed Studio, for instance, we immediately had to download a 49MB(!) patch from the developer's website. This fixed several 'issues'. Within a week, there were two further patches available on the site. Luckily, Studio calls home to check for updates itself so you don't have to remember; but with a 49MB file to download, you're looking at two hours or more on the end of a modem before you can get started.

Indeed, we'll go further. Video editors are notorious for crashing computers, hanging during rendering and failing to complete projects, sometimes wasting hours of computer time in the process and often without any discernible pattern or reason. As we write, both Studio 9 and VideoStudio 8 are new to the market, so we can't comment authoritatively on whether they are trouble-free, but past experience suggests caution.

Check for upgrades as soon as you install your video editor software.

Test your camcorder connection

Before attempting to capture video for the first time, we recommend checking that the camcorder, the FireWire port and the connection cable are all in working order. If you can follow these simple steps, you know that your hardware is up to the task. Please note that this only works for Windows XP.

1

Connect your camcorder to the mains power or run it from a battery but don't turn it on yet. For this test, it doesn't matter whether or not there's a tape in the device. Now connect the camcorder's DV out socket to the computer's FireWire port using the cable supplied.

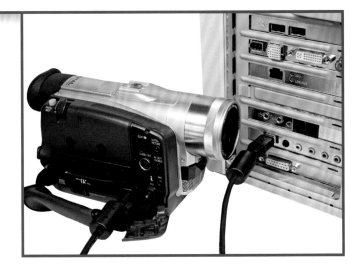

2

Switch on the camcorder. If your speakers are turned on, you'll hear a bing-bong sound effect from Windows and you should be presented with a 'what do you want to do' dialogue box. In future, this will be handy because it allows you to fire up your video editor as soon as the camcorder is connected. Here you can see that Studio has already been installed. For now, though, select the 'no action' option.

3

Open My Computer. Odd though it seems, your digital camcorder now shows up in Windows as a drive-like device. Double-click the camcorder icon.

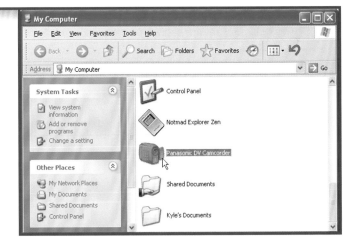

④

In the top part of the camcorder folder, you should see the current view from the camcorder (hint: remove the lens cap). Try taking a picture. What you'll get is a low resolution, probably out of focus, snapshot but the point here is rudimentary testing, not quality photography.

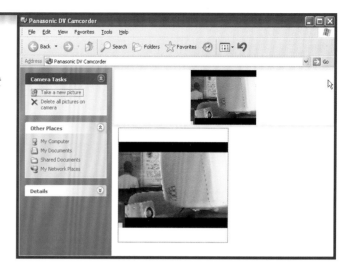

⑤

If you have a tape in the camcorder and it contains some footage, switch the camcorder to VCR/playback mode and use the transport controls. You can now review your recording in this folder window. Again, use the 'take picture' option to capture a low resolution frame.

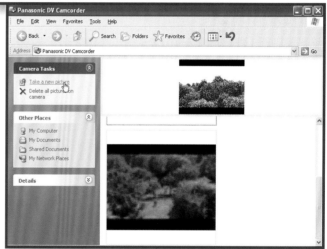

⑥

Now pull the FireWire cable from the camcorder or the computer, or just switch off the camcorder. Its icon will disappear from My Computer and the folder window will close. Pop the cable back in or turn on the camcorder once more, and again you'll hear the bing-bong welcome and be presented with the dialogue box from Step 2. FireWire is a hot-swappable interface, which means you can plug devices in and out at will without having to reboot the computer.

Note that this time around we have an additional choice, as VideoStudio has been recently installed.

PART

Capturing your first video

In the following worked example, we'll capture some video from a digital camcorder using Pinnacle Studio. In fact, we'll run the same procedure three times to highlight the main options.

Some points to note at the outset are:

● The MiniDV tape was 'striped' or 'formatted' (or whatever you want to call it – see p33) before we began shooting. This means it has a continuous timecode, which in turn makes it suitable for accurate scene detection and batch capture.

● During capture, it is important to run the camcorder off mains power or a fully-charged battery. The last thing you want is for it to run out of juice.

Most video capture/editor programs test your hard disk first time around to ensure that it's fast enough for digital video. Don't skip this step.

Full-quality DV AVI capture

First off, we'll capture some footage in the DV AVI format. This is the recommended procedure unless hard disk space is really tight.

1

Connect the camcorder to the computer via FireWire and turn it on. Switch it to VCR/playback mode rather than Camera/record mode. If Windows asks you what you want to do, as here, select your capture program. If not, just launch the program manually.

2

Open the Capture program module. In Studio, the various modules – Capture, Edit and Make Movie – are accessed by means of tabs running across the top of the screen. Note the big picture of a digital camcorder. You'll use this in a moment to control your own camcorder remotely.

3

*Click Setup on the toolbar and then Capture Source.
This dialogue box confirms that the capture source –
i.e. the device with the video – is a digital camcorder.
Now click the folder icon in the Data rate section of this
box and tell Studio where you want to save your
captured video. The default folder is My Videos folder, a
sub-folder of My Documents.*

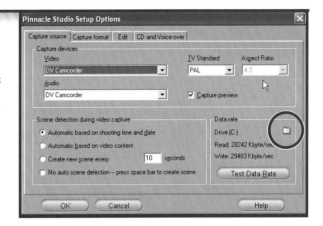

4

*Click Test Data Rate to check that your hard disk is
swift enough to capture digital video. The test only takes
a few moments. So long as your disk passes, which is
likely, proceed. Should it fail, you really need to be
looking at a replacement. See p22 for options.*

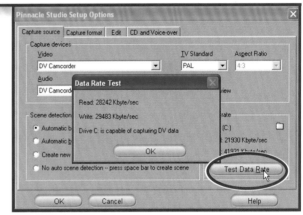

5

*In the scene detection section, you have some options.
Because we are confident that our striped tape has a
continuous timecode, we can select the 'time and date'
option. This means that Studio will create a new scene
every time it detects that recording was paused or
stopped, even if only for a moment. If the tape
timecode is incomplete, Studio may stumble, in which
case you're better off selecting the 'based on video
content' option or bypassing scene detection altogether.*

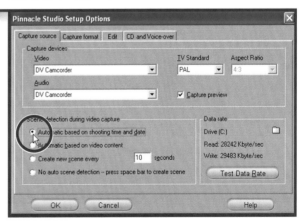

6

*Now open the Capture format tab and ensure that DV
is selected. This is because we want to capture video
from the camcorder in its raw DV AVI format without
applying any further compression. We'll return to these
options in Step 1 on p55. For now, click OK to close the
dialogue box.*

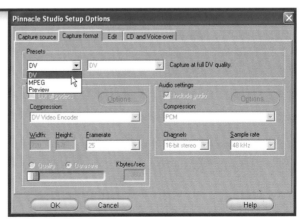

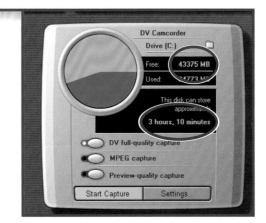

Studio is now primed to capture video from the camcorder to the My Videos folder in the DV AVI format. Note the graphical 'diskometer' lower right which tells you how much free disk space you have on the selected drive (over 43GB here) and how much video that equates to at your chosen capture settings (over 3 hours).

Click the rewind button on Studio's picture of a camcorder and your real camcorder should respond accordingly. When you click Play, you can preview your camcorder footage in Studio's preview window. Note the time display: in this example, 5 minutes, 28 seconds and 3 frames. This is the program reading the timecode from the tape. Cue the tape to the start of the footage you want to capture, or simply rewind to the beginning.

Click the big green button on the diskometer and Studio asks you where to save the captured file. It remembers the folder you selected in Step 3 so there's no need to change this but you should give your file a meaningful name. You can also tell the program how much footage you want to capture, which is useful if you're capturing only part of a tape and you know its rough duration. Leave it at the maximum setting if you'd rather stop the capture process manually.

Studio now takes control of your camcorder and copies the video to the hard disk. Monitor progress in the preview window and stop capturing at any time with the big red button. If you selected automatic scene detection in Step 5, each new scene appears as a thumbnail in the Album (top left). When the process is complete, look in your my Videos folder for a large video file named according to your choice in Step 9 and bearing an AVI extension.

High-quality MPEG-2 capture

This time around, we'll get Studio to encode the camcorder footage as an MPEG file during capture. This dramatically reduces the hard disk space required to store captured video but there's a dual payoff in terms of reduced quality and the time it takes to render the compressed file after editing. By way of comparison, Studio's three options are as follows:

Which you choose depends on which type of disk you intend to make at the end of the production process. If you intend to make a streaming file for the internet, low quality would be the natural choice. There is also a custom mode that lets you dictate your own frame sizes and data rate but that's of little interest.

	File format	Frame size	Data rate
High quality (DVD)	MPEG-2	720 x 576	6,000Kbps
Medium quality (SVCD)	MPEG-2	480 x 576	2,400Kbps
Low quality (Video CD)	MPEG-1	352 x 288	1,150Kbps

Return to the Capture format tab we saw in Step 6 above and make your selection. For purposes of comparison, we'll capture the same video as we did before but this time with MPEG-2 compression applied.

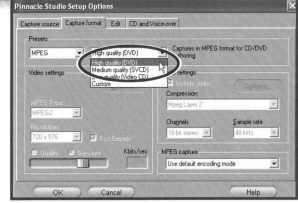

Studio asks whether you want to encode the captured video in real time or after capture. If you select real time, the program will capture and encode in the same operation. However, this requires a fast processor in the 2GHz range and there's a danger of dropping frames. To play it safe, opt for encoding after capture. This guarantees good results even if takes considerably longer. You can also let Studio itself take this decision by selecting 'default encoding mode'. For what it's worth, the program chose to encode in real time on our 2.4GHz PC.

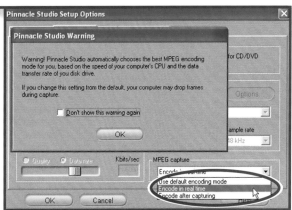

Now repeat Steps 9 and 10 on p54, being sure to give your file a meaningful and original name. Note the diskometer display here: the same hard disk has less free space than it did in Step 7 on p54 but can now capture nearly 14 hours of video compared to 3 hours earlier. That's the beauty of compression.

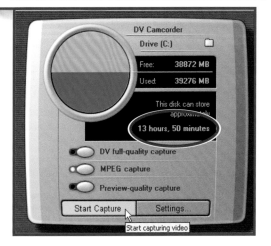

The capture process complete, compare and contrast these two video files on the hard disk. The first was 20 minutes of uncompressed DV AVI capture, weighing in at nearly 4.5GB. The second is the exact same footage encoded in the MPEG-2 format, now a mere 1GB.

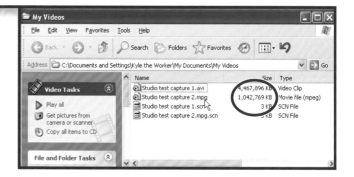

Preview capture

A third alternative is selecting preview capture (or SmartCapture, in Studio's lingo). This is where footage is captured from the camcorder at a low resolution to save on disk space. You can then edit this video just like any other.

Preview capture is inconvenient in the sense that you have to reconnect your camcorder to recapture footage at the end of a project, and it only works at all when there's a continuous timecode on the tape. Any non-striped gaps between recording sessions render SmartCapture helpless. However, because only a limited amount of video need ever be captured as DV AVI, it's certainly an option to consider if your hard disk is close to capacity.

Back to the Capture format screen. The lower the capture quality, the less disk space is required. However, it's important to appreciate that this affects the appearance of your video during editing. When all you have to work with is a grainy, low resolution version of the original, it can be tricky judging when to apply effects and when to make cuts.

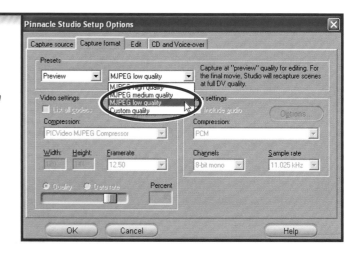

Having run through the same capture process again with these new settings, the file size of the captured footage has now dropped to a remarkable 83MB, or less than 2% of the file size of the original DV AVI capture. With SmartCapture at the helm, our disk now had enough free space to capture 177 hours of video.

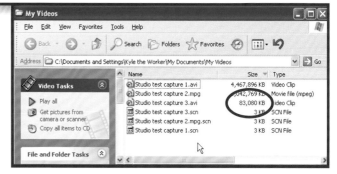

PART

Key differences in VideoStudio

If you have Ulead VideoStudio 8, capturing video from a digital camcorder works in much the same way. VideoStudio has a much larger preview window that can be expanded to full screen even during capture, whereas with Studio you have to be in editing mode before you can resize the screen. VideoStudio also captures and encodes video directly to the WMV file format as well as to the various MPEG-1 and MPEG-2 formats. And, of course, you can capture in 'raw' DV AVI.

However, scene detection is by timecode only, with no option to split scenes automatically according to changes in frame content. Each scene is also saved as a separate video file whereas Studio saves only one file and remembers the splits.

There is no direct SmartCapture equivalent in VideoStudio. Instead, it has a batch capture feature that lets you grab selected scenes from a tape. This is a manual procedure that involves marking in points and out points while previewing the tape. Although it ultimately saves time by not capturing unnecessary footage, it's arguably just as easy to delete superfluous scenes once they're on the hard disk.

VideoStudio in capture mode, controlling a digital camcorder.

PART 3 Watching your captured video

You can play captured video files immediately with a software player. Windows Media Player is as good as any and will handle AVI, MPEG-1 and WMV files without difficulty. However, you'll only be able to play an MPEG-2 file in Windows Media Player if a third-party MPEG-2 codec has been installed on your system.

The first thing you'll notice during playback is, we fear, that your movie doesn't look half as good as you hoped it would. There are two reasons for this.

First, because you are not a professional film-maker and not using professional kit or a crew, your movies are always going to be prone to the odd spot of camera shake, mysterious fluctuations in lighting, focus problems and ropey composition. But most of this can be fixed during editing, and what can't be fixed can be easily discarded. Your captured video and your finished movie will be very different animals, so don't panic yet.

Secondly, though, your computer monitor is a very high resolution progressive scan device, whereas your TV is a low resolution interlaced display. They also handle colours in different

ways. The upshot is that what looks a little dodgy on a monitor can often look just fine on a telly. The difficulty you have during editing is that you won't know just how your movie will look on the big screen until you've burned and played a VCD or DVD, by which time those laborious colour corrections and effects filters might have done more harm than good.

If you can bear the palaver, it pays to connect a portable TV to your computer throughout the editing process, and indeed right at the start when you play your captured files. What you need, apart from a TV, of course, is a means of outputting a video signal from your computer to dual displays. The easiest way by far is if the video card has an S-Video or composite video output alongside its VGA (monitor) output. Depending on the hardware and its support software, you may be able to run the monitor and TV simultaneously, or else you may have to alternate between the two.

Even if your PC doesn't have a video-out socket, you can use the VGA socket if you invest in a signal converter that turns the VGA signal into a composite video or S-Video signal that your TV can understand.

All of this assumes that your TV has a matching S-Video or composite video input. This is the norm on modern TVs but if yours is of a certain age and lacks anything but a SCART socket, what you need is a SCART adapter. This plugs into the TV's SCART socket and lets you connect a composite video or S-Video cable from the computer.

Is it worth it? Well, that's a personal decision. We would simply say that previewing raw captured footage, transitions and especially titles and captions on a TV, even an old portable, gives you a much better idea of the finished project than a monitor screen. A fine, elegant script used for credits or titles may look fantastic from half a metre away on a 19-inch high resolution monitor but be completely illegible when seen on TV from across the room.

This device lets you connect a computer's monitor socket to a TV input.

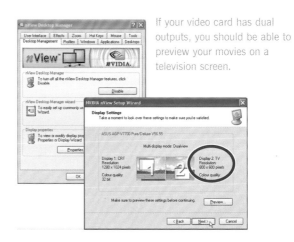

If your video card has dual outputs, you should be able to preview your movies on a television screen.

PART 3

Safeguarding your files

If you're as paranoid about backing up data as we are, now is a good time to make duplicate copies of your captured files. This way, should your hard disk fail or your PC get pinched, you'll be able to recover your videos from the backups. Naturally, if you intend not to reuse the MiniDV tape in your camcorder, you already have a backup: just keep the tape safe and at any time you can capture the source footage afresh. However, tapes are pricey and you may prefer to re-record fresh video. In this case, your only copy of what could be irreplaceable footage – toddler's first steps, Granny's 101st birthday party, a clip destined to fetch £250 on one of those 'world's most mildly amusing pratfalls' shows – now lives on your computer.

The all too obvious problem is that DV AVI video files are huge: up to 13GB per hour. However, if you have a DVD writer drive, you can copy anywhere from 4 to 8GB per disc, depending on whether it (and your recording software) supports the new dual-layer recordable DVD formats. If your captured file is still too big, chop it into chunks that can be reassembled later, and spread it over as many discs as required. Our favourite tool for this kind of task is WinRAR (**www.rarlabs.com**).

Failing all of that, we suggest encoding a copy of the entire captured video without any cuts or effects as a highly compressed MPEG-1 or WMV file. This will shrink it to manageable proportions for copying to CD or DVD. In the worst case, you will now have a playable, albeit relatively low resolution, backup video. See p138-142 for details.

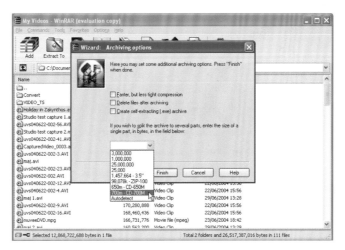

Split your videos into bite-sized chunks for safe-keeping.

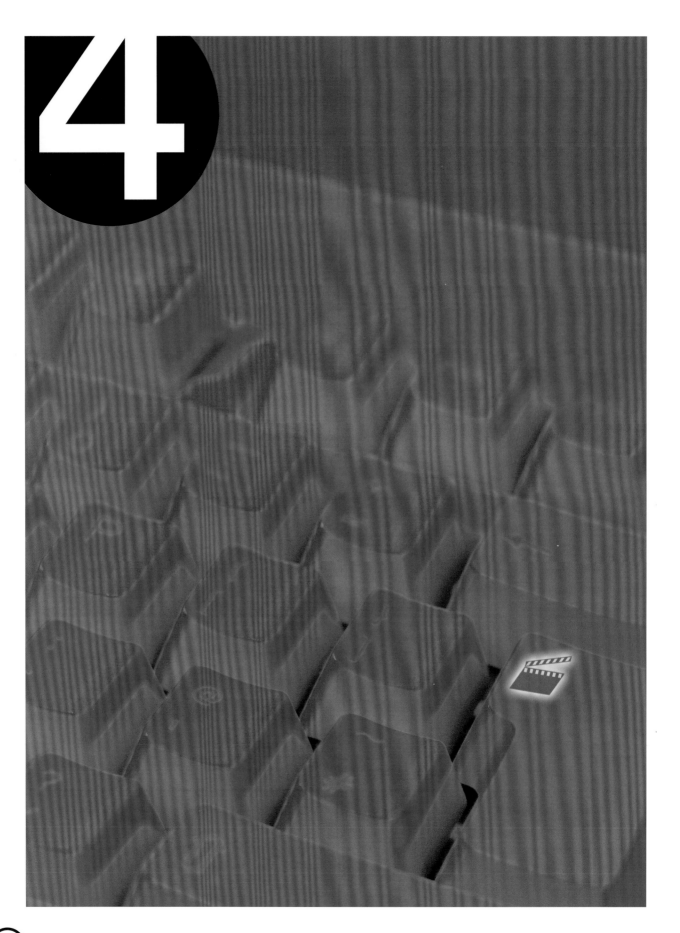

PART **4** **The Storyboard story**

PART 4 Get with the scene

When working with video, it is vital to consider your audience. Let's say you want to produce a memento of your family holiday. You have perhaps four MiniDV tapes, which means up to four hours of raw footage. At best, you'll get an hour's video on a single DVD, and that's plenty. Before you even start, then, you know you'll have to edit your source footage down to a quarter of its size...

But let's be honest: who really wants to sit through even an hour of your holiday? Would you if you hadn't been there? Do you now even though you were? People get bored with a pack of snapshots so have some mercy. Now is the time to consider whether it's worth making two versions of your holiday movie: a long version for the family that preserves every special moment, and a (much) shorter version for friends that captures the essence of your experience. Less is more, in short, and edited highlights are quite enough for all but a captive audience. Your friends will thank you for your brevity.

At the same time, however, we strongly suggest you start off by capturing every last frame of footage. Even that final segment shot on the last day when you'd exhausted your creativity and were reduced to shooting sandcastles in close-up might yield a precious nugget that warrants inclusion. Give yourself the widest possible base from which to start and then be ruthlessly selective. If you want a rule of thumb, we've found that a ratio of 1 minute of finished movie per 10–15 minutes of original footage is about right. That may sound absurdly hard-nosed, and we agree that you'll probably end up cutting scenes purely for reasons of space rather than quality. But that's the nature of the game. Always remember that the audience doesn't miss what the audience doesn't see. A starlit trek through the desert on a camel may have been the experience of a lifetime, but if all you have to show for it is twenty minutes of dark sky punctuated with the odd glimpse of a hairy ear caught in your camcorder's key light... well, a film editor's life is full of tough decisions.

If your friends and family shudder when you gather them round for another home movie extravaganza, you need to learn the art of judicious cutting.

PART **4** Building a story

Any video editor worth the purchase price offers two quite distinct editing modes: storyboard and timeline. Even Movie Maker does this, and it's free. When you're first starting out, you'll work primarily, perhaps exclusively, with storyboards; but when you need fine control, you'll turn to the timeline. We'll look at these in turn. But first…

During the video capture process described earlier, we saw individual scenes being created on the fly. These scene splits may be just where you want them. However, it's much more likely that some scenes are too long and others contain snippets of footage that you'd rather weren't there. Very few of us ever master the art of shooting the perfect scene from start to finish. But of course we don't have to. That's the beauty of a 'non-linear' video editor like Studio, VideoStudio, Movie Maker 2, Premiere Pro or just about any of the other programs out there.

After capture, the first step in computer-based movie-making is the broad stroke business of manipulating scenes and imposing structure. The idea is to emerge with a coherent story in which every scene plays a part, and plays it well. (That's if you want coherence, mind – if not, skip to Appendix 3 now.)

As you know, all good (conventional) stories have a beginning, a middle and an end. Trite though it sounds, it's something to hold onto when structuring your movie. A shot of a fraught queue at the airport merging into a glorious sunny beach scene is as good a way as any of starting a holiday movie; a wave from the hotel balcony at sundown makes a suitable, if corny, ending. In between, include the best highlights of your holiday. However, don't feel obliged to stick with strict chronology. Nobody but you knows what you did when, and you might find you can make a better movie by juxtaposing non-consecutive scenes. Try to approach the project as an objective editor would, even when you're the star of the show.

Again, we're working with Pinnacle Studio. Whatever software you use, the storyboard principles are the same.

A comic strip is basically a storyboard. Feel free to find inspiration wherever you can.

First things first: from the File menu, start a new project, give it a name, and remember to save it frequently (video editing software is renowned for instability and random crashes). This way, Studio will remember all your edits and you can close and reopen a project as you go along. Note that your original captured footage is not altered in any way during editing, so you can always scrub a project and start all over again. You can also have several concurrent projects based on the same captured footage.

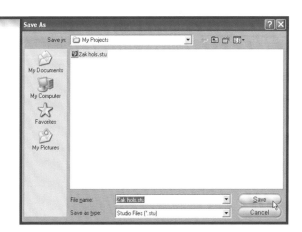

2

Open the Edit module and find your captured video. If you have just finished capturing footage from your camcorder, the newly saved video will already be open in the Album; if not, use the folder icon on the left page of the Album to navigate to it now. You'll find it in the folder you selected in Step 3 on p53, with the file name you selected in Step 9.

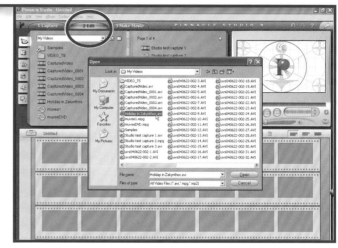

3

It's possible to import any video (in a supported file format) at this stage, not just your own captured footage. When you select such a file, Studio runs scene detection on it just as if it was captured footage. This takes some time, although you can always click Cancel to stop detection and import the file as a single clip.

4

If you allowed Studio to detect scenes during capture or when importing a file, these scenes now appear as thumbnails in the Album. You may have several pages of scenes – here we have nine double-page spreads – in which case use the little arrows on the pages to flip between them.

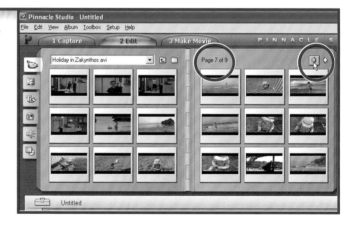

5

Click once on any thumbnail in the Album to select that scene. To play it, use the transport controls (play, fast forward, rewind etc.) under the preview window to the right of the album. Unless you pause or stop playback, Studio will play each scene consecutively. In the Album, the scene that's currently being played is always highlighted.

Note the slider at the bottom of the preview window. This shows you where you are relative to the entire video. for instance, if you're currently playing one of the middle scenes, the slider will be in the middle. Drag it to the left or right to zoom to different points in the video. The Album keeps pace by flicking pages, always highlighting the current scene.

In the Album, each scene is depicted as a thumbnail that displays the first frame in that scene. But sometimes this won't be an accurate representation of the scene's main theme or content. No problem. Select the scene in the Album, play it in the preview window, and pause on a frame that sums it up. Then right-click the scene in the Album and select Set Thumbnail.

While watching the video in the preview window, click the little arrow below and to the right of the window. It will now play full screen, which is essential if you have a TV connected to your computer as a second monitor. To return to the standard Studio view, hit the Escape key.

A word about aspect ratios. Right-click any scene and see whether 4:3 or 16:9 is checked. Here we can see that Studio is working on the assumption that this video is 16:9, which accounts for the letterbox-shaped preview window. However, as we mentioned earlier, many camcorders include a faux-16:9 feature that superimposes black bands top and bottom on a 4:3 frame. That's how this footage was shot but the effect appears to have fooled Studio into treating it as genuinely 16:9. Thus the frames are stretched horizontally to fill a 16:9 ratio, which accounts for the extreme letterboxing and distortion in the previous step. To correct this, we can change the aspect ratio back to 4:3. This only has to be done once with any scene in the Album: the entire project will then adopt the correct 4:3 ratio.

Repeat Step 8 to play the video full screen again. This time, with the project now adjusted to the correct 4:3 aspect ratio, we still have the black bands imposed by the camcorder but we've lost the additional stretching imposed on the footage by Studio. This is how the footage was originally shot, this is how it should be seen, and this is how it should be edited.

The Storyboard forms the lower half of Studio's Edit module. Select any scene from any page in the Album, and drag and drop it onto the Storyboard. It will automatically land in the first 'slot'. Alternatively, right-click any Album thumbnail and select Add to Project. This scene now becomes a 'clip' in your movie project proper. It still appears as a thumbnail in the Album view but it's now flagged with a green tick to mark its special status. To remove a clip from the Storyboard, right-click it and select Delete (or click on it once to select it and hit the Delete key).

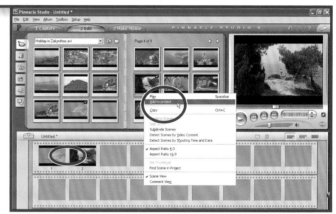

Add a few new clips to your storyboard by plucking scenes from anywhere in the Album. When you have perhaps 5 or 6 in place, drag and drop them into a new order. To do this, select a clip and drag it to the left or right. A vertical green marker appears between adjacent clips to show you where it will 'land'. Now select the first clip in the Storyboard and play the entire project. Reorder clips as often as you like, and add and remove clips as you see fit.

A good point at which to save the project. Doing so means you can return to this point in the future and carry on exactly where you left off. Once again we emphasise that nothing you have done so far affects your original captured video: it's still sitting there safe and unchanged on the hard disk. Studio has simply kept track of changes that might be made at some point in the future.

PART 4 Trimming and splitting clips

Once you have a project underway and a few clips in your storyboard, you can begin to fine-tune your movie. At this stage, the best approach is working with one clip at a time, tweaking each into something approaching perfection. Let's run through the options now.

Before we start, we should stress that you get an infinite number of attempts to get your movie right. If at any time you regret trimming or splitting a clip, just delete the edited versions from the Storyboard and start with a fresh scene plucked from the Album. And if it all goes horribly wrong, simply start a new project and begin all over again, using the same captured (or imported) video as your source material.

1

Three routes to the Clip Properties screen:
- *Select a scene in the Storyboard and click the Toolbox icon (located at the far left end of the toolbar just above the Storyboard)*
- *Right-click a scene in the Storyboard and select Clip Properties*
- *Double-click a scene in the Storyboard*

This is where you trim clips.

2

Here we can see a clip open in Clip Properties. In the left window is the first frame; in the right window, the last. The clip also has its own mini-timecode – this clip is just over 18 seconds long – and we can drag the slider to view any part of it. Clip Properties also has its own transport controls. For full control, pause the video and use the arrows next to the time code to advance and retreat the clip one frame at a time.

3

This particular clip shows some roundabout action. That's all very jolly but we don't really want 18 seconds of it in our movie. To trim the clip, use the sliding markers to set the in and out points. In this example, the clip will start just as the girl emerges waving from behind the tree and will end some seven seconds later when she has completed a full revolution. Use the transport controls to preview your trimmed clip then close the clip toolbox by clicking the cross in the top-right corner.

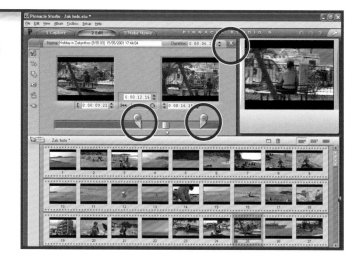

4

Sometimes, a clip may have two or more sequences of interest but with some duff stuff in between. There are two ways to proceed here. First, and easiest, drag two copies of the same scene into the Storyboard and trim each accordingly. In this screenshot, clips 1 and 2 were identical but we've trimmed the first to show the opening beach scene and we're now trimming the second to grab a short sequence from later on in the same clip.

5

The alternative approach is to split a clip at any defined point. This effectively turns it into two clips which can thereafter be treated entirely independently. Select a clip in the Storyboard and play it in the main preview window. Use the pause button to freeze the frame at roughly the split point, and click the up and down arrow buttons next to the timecode to move through the video a frame at a time. Hone in on your precise split point and click the Split Clip button located on the toolbar above the Storyboard. You now have two adjacent clips in the Storyboard. If you don't like the result, click Edit > Undo Split clip to restore the original clip (or delete both clips from the Storyboard and start again).

PART 4 Transitions

A transition is a way of moving from one scene in a movie to another. The natural, default transition in any project is a hard cut, which is to say an abrupt transition between clip A and clip B.

Very often, that's also the most appropriate transition. Watch any TV programme or movie and you'll see that hard cuts are the norm. However, a video editor gives you some – actually, many – additional options. You can fade one scene out and fade the next scene in, dissolve the dying frames of one scene into the opening frames of the next, have a fresh scene 'push' the current scene out of the picture, or have a scene crumple like paper, float off in a balloon or disappear with the flick of a virtual page.

Scene transitions are a great way to add an extra dynamic to your videos and can be used to great effect. For instance, when moving from footage of a couple saying their wedding vows to a clip of them signing the register, a simple fade out/fade in transition provides an obvious and appropriate break between two discrete yet related scenes. It also affords the viewer a pause, or a breathing space.

Unfortunately, transitions tempt the amateur movie maker into the most horrendous mistakes. Nothing, but nothing, ruins a good video like superfluous, flashy scene transitions. Just because you have a hundred possibilities to choose from doesn't mean you have to use them all. It doesn't mean you have to use

any. Treat transitions with the same rigour that you apply to trimming clips and only replace a hard cut with something fancier when it genuinely adds something to the story.

This advice is particularly true of 3-D transitions. Some of these are truly impressive but mostly they just draw attention to themselves and, in consequence, detract from the meat of the movie. Besides, do you really need a pink, pulsating love-heart shot through with an animated arrow to convey the notion of affection between bride and groom?

In short, take it easy with transitions.

One factor to bear in mind is the way in which transitions can affect clip length. Let's say you have two consecutive five-second clips with a hard cut between them. Let's now imagine that you apply a two-second dissolve transition. For this to work, clips A and B have to overlap in order that the final frames of clip A and the opening frames of clip B merge to create the effect. The net result is that you end up with eight seconds of video. In contrast, you could apply a two-second fade-out to clip A and a two-second fade-in to clip B and still have ten seconds of video.

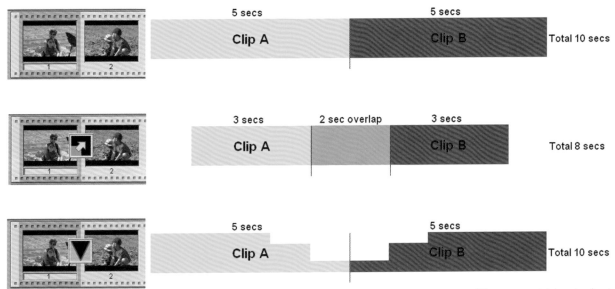

When you maintain a hard cut or apply a fade in/fade out transition between two clips, nothing is lost. But when you use any transition in which the clips merge, the clips overlap and so the combined length is shortened.

1

In Studio's Edit module, click the Transitions tab just to the left of the Album. It opens at the Standard Transitions screen with three double-page spreads to choose from. Select any transition with a click and you can watch the effect in the preview window.

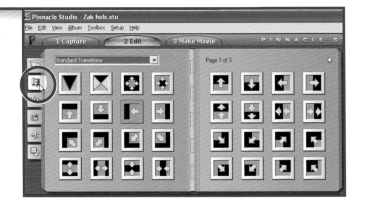

2

Studio also ships with an additional collection of transitions known as Hollywood FX that can be accessed via the drop down menu in the Album. However, only the 'Hollywood FX for Studio' collection comes free; the others, many of which are fantastical exercises in 3-D animation, are stamped with a watermark and you have to pay up to 'unlock' them. Is it worth it? You decide.

3

Back with the standard transitions, drag one down to the Storyboard, position it between two clips – the outline of a green square appears to show you where it will land – and drop it in place.

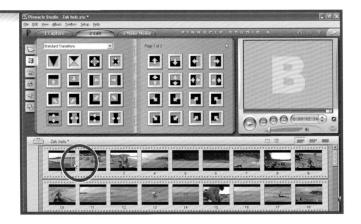

4

The transition now appears as an icon between the two clips in the Storyboard. Check the effect by selecting the first clip and playing it in the preview window. Here, the second clip emerges through the centre of the first clip.

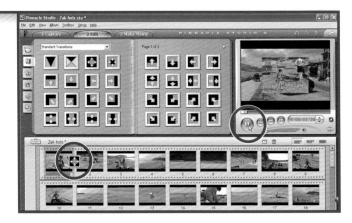

5

In Studio, the default duration for most transitions is two seconds. This is about right most of the time, although you might prefer a longer fade between 'chapters' in a movie. Double-click a transition in the Storyboard (or right-click it and select Clip Properties, or click the Toolbox icon on the toolbar). The Clip Properties window now opens in place of the Album.

6

Your options here are simple. In the duration field top right, you can change the length of the transition. By checking the Reverse box, you can run the effect backwards (this doesn't alter the order of the clips, of course). Preview any changes with the transport controls. Do bear in mind that if you increase the duration of a transition, a longer proportion of each clip is tied up in the effect.

7

To remove a transition, right-click it in the Storyboard and select Delete. To copy it, right-click it and select Copy; and to paste that copy elsewhere, right-click any clip and select Paste. To move a transition to a different position in the project, drag and drop it along the Storyboard. Note that when you copy or move a transition, any edits are carried with it.

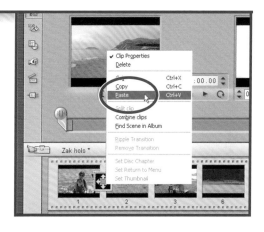

8

One appropriate place for a transition is right at the start of a movie project. Drag and drop a transition just to the left of the first clip in your Storyboard and it will drop in place. A relatively long transition of five or six seconds works well, as your movie will gradually fade – or swirl, or peel, or burst – into view from a black background. You'll sacrifice the first few seconds of footage, though, so make an allowance for this when trimming the clip.

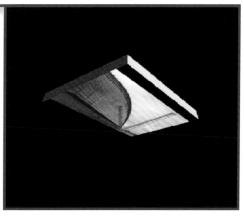

PART  # Titles and captions

One of the most pleasing aspects of making your own movies is being able to add text to the video. You know the kind of thing: a caption pops up to describe a certain scene ('One day, we will buy this castle!'), titles introduce the beginning of new chapters ('Day 7: We headed inland...'), and credits fore and aft add a little self-congratulatory personalisation. This kind of thing is much easier than you might expect and, when used sparingly, is highly effective.

Not convinced? Let's take a look.

At the very simplest level, Studio offers a small range of caption templates. To access these, click the Title tab to the left of the Album. You can now select any caption and view it in the preview window. Note that each caption has a default duration.

Drag any caption onto any clip in the Storyboard. Now select that clip and play it in the preview window. Hey presto: instant captioning. The caption kicks in with the first frame and 'plays' for the default duration we saw in Step 1.

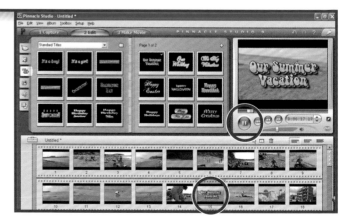

3

If you want a caption to appear midway through a clip rather than right at the start, the easiest thing to do is to split the clip at the key frame. We looked at splitting clips back on p67. Now drag the caption onto the second of the split clips. During playback, the split between clips is completely transparent so the caption will pop up midway through what appears to be a continuous scene.

4

To delete a caption from a clip, open the relevant clip in Clip Properties box as before (see Step 1 on p67). At this stage, there's no sign of the caption, which is a little disconcerting, but now click the Title tab to the left. The caption appears in isolation. Click the Edit Title button.

5

To delete the caption, click once anywhere on the lettering and the entire caption will be bounded by a grey hatched line (in fact, it should be pre-selected when you first open this screen). Click anywhere on this hatched line and it will change to a solid line. This means that the caption has been selected. Either press the Delete key on your keyboard or use the trash can icon in the toolbar below the main window to remove the caption. Now click OK to return to the Storyboard view.

It's probably worth mentioning that it's much easier working with (and deleting) captions in the Timeline view, as we'll see.

Designing your own captions

In the previous section, you could have paused at Step 5 to edit the caption instead of deleting it. However, you can also create your own captions from scratch in the same way.

In extreme cases, you may not be able to preview the finished effect of a caption in all its glory until the project is rendered. This depends mainly on the speed of your computer, and is most likely when you create a moving caption that spans several clips. The program simply can't work fast enough to show you the end result in the preview window in real time. Remember to save your project as you go along so you never have to repeat any editing should the program crash or hang.

1

To get to the Title Editor straight from the Storyboard, select the clip to which you want to apply a caption, open Clip Properties, and click the Title tab. You now have two options: Title Overlay or Full Screen Title. The first is a caption that appears 'on top' of the video, like the 'Our Summer Vacation' example we've been working with; and the second is essentially a still frame with no underlying video. In either case, the principles are the same. Here we'll start with a full screen title.

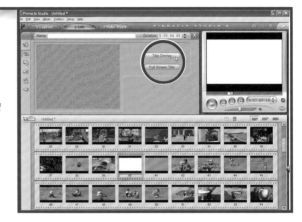

2

The opening blank canvas doesn't look particularly inspiring but it will be familiar territory to anybody who's worked with desktop publishing or even played around with formatted text options in a word processor. You can start designing from almost any angle but here we've clicked the Backgrounds button. This opens a sidebar with a few background designs. Click one and it fills the entire design window.

3

Alternatively, use the solid colour or gradient buttons located just above the background designs to choose a coloured background. The gradient fill button shown here lets you merge four colours in a gently blended palette.

4

You can also use a still picture as a background. Click the Camera button to the left of the sidebar and use the Folder button to browse your hard disk. Rather oddly, when you home in on a single image and open it, any other images stored in the same folder are automatically displayed as thumbnails in the sidebar.

5

Double-click an image or drag it into the preview window. Now click on it once to select it, and drag it out to the appropriate dimensions. Here we have moved the image to the top left corner – click and hold anywhere inside the image to drag it – and then 'grabbed' the resize handle on the picture's lower right corner. We can now stretch it to fill the screen.

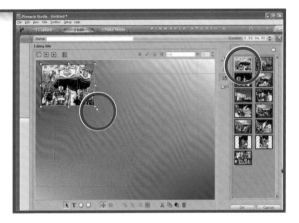

6

Like this. In fact, you can use several images for a compound effect and arrange them however you like, including in layers. Beware of fussiness, though. Meanwhile, we're going to delete this image. Select any item in the main screen by clicking on it, at which point it becomes bounded by a frame. When thus selected, press the Delete key or use the trash can icon to remove it.

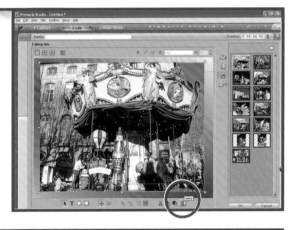

Back at a plain but multi-coloured background, let's now add some text. Click the Text Box button on the toolbar at the bottom of the screen and click anywhere in the preview window. This generates a text box, which is basically a container for holding and moving text. Click and drag the yellow handles to make the text box as big as you like. To move it around the screen, move the mouse cursor inside the box; when it changes to a double-headed arrow, click, hold and drag.

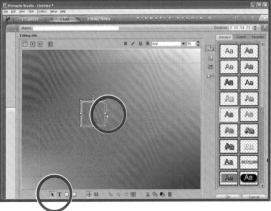

8

Here we have made a rectangular text box and positioned it close to the top of the screen. Now click the text button on the sidebar and explore the Standard tab to see more possibilities. Point at a style and you'll get a popup box with a few related variations. Click on one of these now to select a font style and colour. You can also use the Custom tab to change the properties of any style.

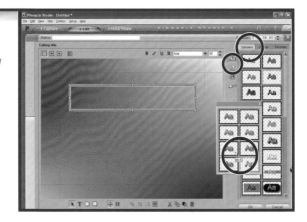

9

Start typing. Your words will appear in the text box and, if necessary, the box will expand to accommodate them. You can treat this text just as you would in a word processor. To change the font style and colour, for instance, highlight the text with the mouse cursor and use the format buttons above and to the right of the preview window.

10

When you're finished, click anywhere outside the text box to de-select it. This is how your full screen caption will appear in the video. At the very top right of the screen is the duration field. The default is four seconds, but alter this as you see fit. Finally, click OK. Your caption now appears as a clip in the Storyboard and can be previewed, moved around, copied and pasted or deleted just like any other. To return to the Title Editor, just double-click the caption in the Storyboard.

11

Returning to Step 1 now, click the Title Overlay button. The key difference here is that the caption appears as a transparent layer over the live clip. Adjust the duration to determine how long the caption stays on screen. If the caption duration is longer than the clip, it simply overruns into the next clip. The caption will appear during the first frame of the selected clip, so split a clip at the appropriate point if you want it to start at any other point in the scene.

Note the three buttons grouped together top left of the preview window. The first of these, Title, is the default, and equates to static text. The next one, Roll, causes text to roll up the screen from top to bottom during playback, just like movie credits. The third button, Crawl, makes the caption scroll across the screen from right to left. Be sure to position your text box appropriately i.e. if you place it at the top of the screen, the crawl effect will run horizontally there; if you place it to the left or right, the roll effect will be off-centre.

If you like, adjust the duration of the caption. You don't want a rolling or scrolling caption to fly past in a split second but nor do you want it to linger on screen for too long. When you first create a caption, Studio allocates a default duration which is just long enough for the text to roll or crawl across the screen at a standard pace. If you adjust this, the roll/crawl will be correspondingly slowed down or speeded up.

Note that it's perfectly possible to paste text into a text box from another application, such as a word processor. You might, for instance, want to write your credits in Word and copy them across in one move. Don't worry if the text doesn't all fit in the text box, as Studio accommodates it regardless. It also stretches rolling or crawling captions over as many clips as are required to display the text at the right pace (unless you've manually altered the duration in Step 13). In this case, you'll see the same caption appear as an overlay in each of the affected Storyboard clips. Here, a long (or slow) crawling caption spans three clips.

If you want to run motion credits on a static background at the beginning or end of your movie (rather than overlaid on the video while it is still playing), the easiest way is to drop a standard title (see p72) into its own placeholder at the far end of the Storyboard. It thus becomes a clip in its own right rather than a caption within a clip. Double-click it to open the Title Editor, change the background, replace the text with your own, decide whether you want the credits to roll or crawl, set the duration, and so forth. When we look at audio later, you'll also be able to enhance your credits with a soundtrack.

PART  Working with frame grabs

You can use still images in your video project at any point. You might, for instance, want to include some pictures taken on your digital camera in your holiday movie. If you're making a wedding video, you could scan a couple of the official wedding photographs and use them as title backgrounds. Perhaps you just want to focus the viewer's attention for a few seconds on a particularly good still frame grabbed from a video clip.

Starting with the last suggestion, capturing a still frame is actually very simple. Here's how to do it in Studio.

Still in the Storyboard view, double-click the clip that contains the frame you want to grab. This opens the familiar Clip Properties screen. Now click the frame grabber tool button on the left. It's the one fourth from the top.

In the preview window, use the transport controls to find the precise frame. The easiest way is to play the clip until you get to roughly the right point, then pause. Now use the up and down arrows adjacent to the timecode field to move forward or backwards one frame at a time.

3

Click the Grab button in the frame grabber window and either save the image to the hard disk or insert it straight into your movie. We will save it. This image can now be opened in any image editor for tweaking, or could be emailed or printed. It's basically a rough and ready way of extracting stills from a video.

4

Here we can see the image open in Paint Shop Pro, an image editor program. Note that the image size is 768 x 576 pixels. This is the standard frame size for PAL video, so this makes perfect sense as it was culled from a PAL project.

5

Back in Studio, click the Add to Movie button seen in Step 3 instead of (or in addition to) saving the frame to disk. The frame now becomes a clip in the Storyboard and you can treat it just like any other (drag it to a new position, copy and paste it elsewhere, edit it, delete it, etc.). It also appears as an item in the Album, which is now open at the still images page.

6

Double-click the still frame in the Storyboard and you'll find yourself back at the Title Editor. Now you can overlay a static or moving caption on the image and, importantly, alter the duration of the clip (the default is four seconds). Click OK when you're through.

7

Let's imagine that you wanted to edit the still frame before inserting it into the video. Here, back in Paint Shop Pro, we've transformed the grabbed frame into a negative (probably not a great idea but it helps to make the point in the next step) and saved it with a new file name.

8

In Studio, click the camera button to open the Album at the still images page, and use the folder buttons to navigate to the folder containing the saved image from Step 7. If the folder contains more than one image, Studio automatically imports them all as Album thumbnails.

9

As we can see here. This particular folder has two images: the original still frame that we grabbed and saved in Step 3, and the edited version from Step 7. You can now drag either of these images into any position in the Storyboard and modify it with the Clip Properties or Title Editor tools. Indeed, you can also apply special effects to still frames just as easily as to video clips (see p100).

10

This time, we've opened a folder containing still images taken on a digital camera but saved as files on the hard disk. Any of these can be added to any project, as indeed can just about any image whatsoever, including scans of photographs or pictures downloaded from the internet. The problem, as this screenshot illustrates, is that your raw images may not fit the video frame. This is why we need to look at a little upfront image preparation.

PART 4 Working with still images

When you grab a frame from a video clip, its dimensions naturally match those of the video and thus it is perfectly matched with the project. You can include it without fear of distortion. However, if you import any other images, you may not get quite what you expected.

It comes down to matching aspect ratios, by which we mean that the height and width of an image should bear the same relation to one another as those of the frames of the video. For instance, if you're working with a 4:3 video project, each frame is 1.33 times as wide as it is high; in a 16:9 project, each frame is 1.78 times as wide as it is high (hence the widescreen effect).

When you try to import a portrait-style image, it will look something like the screenshot in Step 10 above i.e. with black bands bordering it on either side. Worse, though, is when you import a landscape image that doesn't have quite the same aspect ratio as the video. In this case, it will end up being distorted as Studio stretches or squashes the image to fill the frame.

The way around the issue is simply to resize your images to the appropriate aspect ratio before you import them into a video project, cropping if necessary. The good news is that most printed snapshots and digital camera images adhere to the 4:3 format, so tweaking often isn't required. But here's how to convert a portrait image to a 4:3 landscape image suitable for inclusion in a 4:3 project. Any image editor can handle this. We happen to be using Paint Shop Pro.

One thing to watch is that you save your images only in a file format that your video editor supports.

Here's the original portrait image. Paint Shop Pro has a resize tool that lets you resize images in several ways. We've unchecked the maintain aspect ratio box and entered the new dimensions for the image in the Pixel Size fields (768 x 576, because we want to match the project video size that we saw in Step 4 on p79).

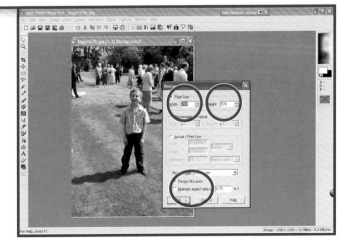

2

Whoops. We forgot that the image was in portrait format. The image is now correctly sized for our video project but all we've achieved is a dramatic squashing of the original image. Time for an undo.

3

This time, we'll use the crop tool. At the bottom left of the screen, Paint Shop Pro displays the pixel size and aspect ratio of the crop area as you move the tool around. By overlaying a rough crop rectangle on the image, it's possible – easy, even – to drag it out until you have selected the best possible area that conforms to an aspect ratio of 1.33 (i.e. 4:3). For a 16:9 project, you should resize to 1.78. The closer you zoom, the more control you have over the crop area, right down to individual pixels.

4

Make the crop. Here we've emerged with a landscape image in which the subject has not been distorted. The actual image size is 1153 x 867 pixels, which equates to an aspect ratio of 4:3. While this not identical to the video frame size of 768 x 576, it's the relationship between height and width that matters. The video editor will simply enlarge or shrink the image to fill the frame when you insert it into the project.

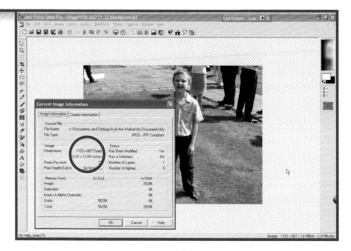

PART  Including a slideshow

As well as using the odd image here and there in a movie, you might care to include a self-contained sequence of snapshots. This can prove quite an effective way of bringing an otherwise monotonous video to life.

Studio has a rather nice feature called 'ripple transition', which we'll explore now.

1 *Place a few still images together on the Storyboard. If you're content with a four-second duration for each clip, fine: if not, open one or all in the clip properties screen and alter the duration. Note that if you double-click a still image clip, you get the Title Editor screen by default. For Clip Properties, use the Clip Properties command from the right-click menu or click the toolbox button.*

2 *Return to the Storyboard and click the Transitions tab to the left of the Album. As you did on p70, drag and drop a transition between the first and second still image clips. Preview the effect in the preview window.*

3 *Now click the second clip to select it, hold down the Control key, and click each subsequent clip in the sequence. This selects them simultaneously. Right-click any one of these selected clips and choose Ripple Transition from the popup menu. The transition you applied in Step 2 is now automatically applied to the entire sequence, and you should have a smooth slideshow. The alternative, of course, is to apply transitions manually between each image, in which case you can have some variety, or simply to leave them as hard cuts.*

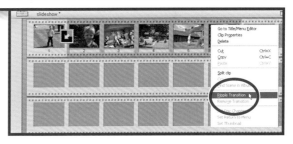

4 *One thing you can't do, unfortunately, is set up a crawling or rolling caption that spans the slideshow (or rather, you can but not from the Storyboard: see p91 for the solution). But what you can do is apply a caption to each clip in turn. The overall effect is much the same. For instance, this clip has a crawling caption ('While the guests had their pictures taken…') and the next clip has a separate but related caption ('…we went mad in the garden!').*

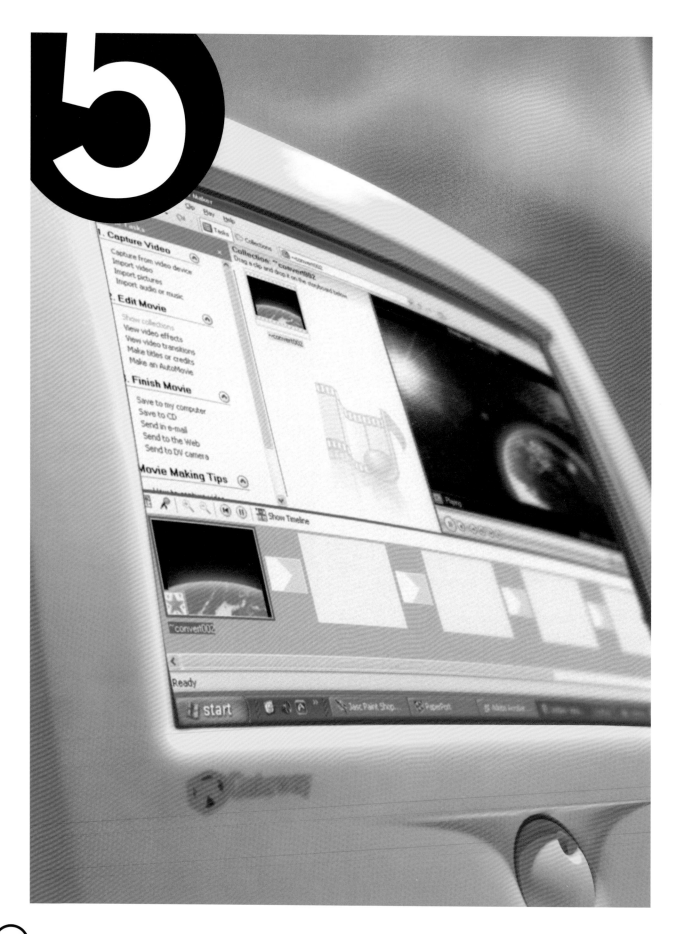

PART **5** # Time for the Timeline

PART 5 Understanding tracks

The beauty of the Storyboard is twofold: it's an extremely intuitive, visual drag-and-drop way of compiling a movie; and you can do just about anything with it.

Just about but not quite. Certain tasks require the Timeline. This is an alternative way of compiling a project in which the various elements that comprise a movie are separated out and displayed in tracks that can be edited individually. The Timeline is a less visual medium than the Storyboard but it's far more flexible.

In a movie, there are a number of tracks. At the simplest level, which is pretty much Studio territory, there are five separate tracks:

● **Video** This track is home to your video clips. That is, when you drag and drop a scene or a still image from the Album into a movie project, this is where it lives. There is only one video track so only one video can play at any one time. The key to the Timeline, as the name suggests, is that clips are represented in terms of their duration, both in absolute terms and relative to one another. A ten-second clip is thus twice as 'long' in the Timeline as a five-second clip.

● **Original audio** When you shoot video on your camcorder, sound is also recorded. When you capture video to your computer, that soundtrack is also transferred. When you play a captured video clip, the soundtrack plays along in synch with the pictures. In the Storyboard view, you can't actually see the soundtrack: it's 'just there'. But in the Timeline, the soundtrack is separated from the video and given its own track.

● **Titles** This is the track used for titles and captions when they are created in Title Overlay mode (see p74). Anything in this track plays 'on top' of the concurrent video clip. This makes it possible to superimpose text and effects on a video despite having just the one dedicated video track.

● **Sound effects/narration** A separate audio track reserved for additional sound effects and/or recorded narration. Anything added here gets mixed with the original soundtrack during production.

● **Background music** Yet another audio track, this time dedicated to background music such as tracks 'ripped' from CDs or MP3 files on your computer. Again, a mix is a must.

Your finished movie is an amalgam of some or all of these tracks. For example, any given scene could encompass video with an underlying soundtrack plus an overlaid caption with added narration and background music. And you thought making home movies was a case of pointing and shooting your digital camcorder?

Incidentally, not all video editors offer the same arrangement of tracks. Movie Maker 2 has only one additional audio track over and above the original soundtrack, so you can add narration or music but not both at the same time. VideoStudio goes further than Studio by letting you add video clips, not just titles and captions, to an overlay track, so it's possible to have two videos running at the same time. We'll look at the possibilities with this on p110.

Meanwhile, let's do some practical, profitable work with the Timeline.

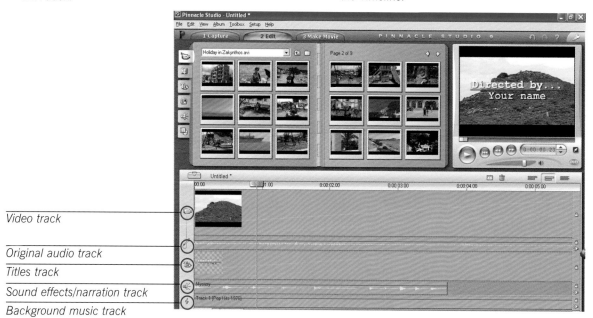

Video track

Original audio track

Titles track

Sound effects/narration track

Background music track

PART  Timeline editing

In the following worked example, we will explore several aspects of editing a movie in Timeline mode rather than in the Storyboard. Indeed, for some things, the Timeline is the only way to work. However, we still prefer to compose a project on the Storyboard in the first instance, as it's the easier way to shuffle video clips around in order to impose a broad structure.

Our starting point here is a short project that includes a few video clips, a couple of still images, scene transitions between them and a crawling caption at the start.

Here we have the project in the familiar Storyboard mode. A crawling caption has been overlaid on clip 1 and overlaps into clip 2. Clip 6 is a still image. Now click the Timeline button on the toolbar above the Storyboard.

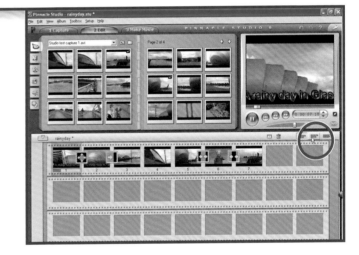

The same project viewed in the Timeline. Each clip is now displayed as a linear container, the length of which represents its duration relative to every other clip and measured precisely according to a timecode running along the top. For instance, the first two clips are both over 20 seconds long whereas the latter clips are clearly shorter.

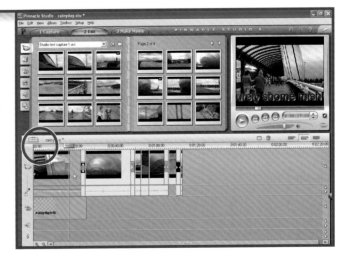

3

Click anywhere on the yellow timecode and the mouse cursor changes to a clock with double arrows. Holding down the left mouse button, drag the cursor to the right to increase the scale of the timecode and to the left to reduce it. This lets you zoom in on particular segments of the project for editing. Here, for instance, we have expanded the timecode sufficiently to see the first two clips in more detail. Using the timecode, we know that the first transition kicks in after 23 seconds and lasts for the default 2 seconds. You can also use the + and minus keys on your keyboard to zoom in on the Timeline.

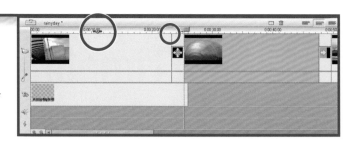

4

Zoomed out again for a moment, what else can we see? Well, for one thing, the opening caption is longer than the duration of the first clip which is why it overlaps with the second clip during playback. For another, there appear to be gaps in the original audio track during scene transitions. This is actually misleading, as in practice clip soundtracks are merged during scene transitions just like the video. With one exception...

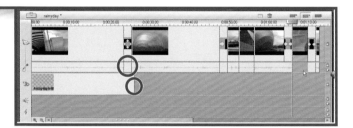

5

Open the Transitions page of the Album and drag a fade transition between the first two clips in the Timeline (you can drag and drop clips and effects from the Album to the Timeline just as easily as to the Storyboard). Now click the first clip to highlight it and, while holding down the control key, click the transition and the second clip. This selects them simultaneously. Note that the original audio track now has a blue line running through it. This represents the volume level. Here, because we have a fade effect, it dips away to nothing mid-transition and then fades back in again.

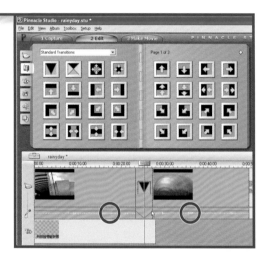

6

When an overlapping transition is highlighted, as here, we can see from the volume level marker that the soundtracks overlap during the transition. The result is a gradual, natural switch of sound from one clip to the next. In a hard cut, of course, the audio track switches between clips as abruptly as the video. We'll be working much more with audio tracks later.

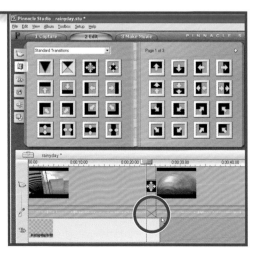

7

Click on the slider in the timecode bar and drag it to the left and to the right. This whisks you through the movie far faster than you can navigate in the Storyboard. The vertical marker shows you where you are relative to the project as a whole, and the current frame is displayed in the preview window. When you use the transport controls in the preview window to play, fast forward or rewind the project, the Timeline's slider and marker keep pace. Use the scroll bar at the very bottom of the screen to navigate through a project that's too long to fit on screen.

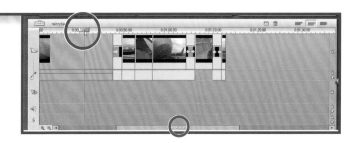

8

Here we have zoomed in on a still image in the video track. Note that the original audio track is completely blank for these four seconds. This is something to be aware of: still images can be used to dramatic effect in a movie but it's decidedly off-putting for the viewer if an otherwise noisy soundtrack suddenly drops off to nothing.

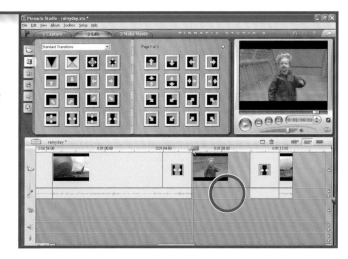

9

We looked earlier at trimming clips with the clip properties tools, but you can also trim a clip directly in the Timeline. Let's say that the first clip is five seconds too long. Zoom in until you can clearly see the timecode, select the clip with a click, and click on the right-hand edge of the clip box. The cursor becomes a left-pointing arrow.

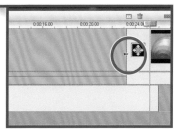

10

Keeping the mouse button depressed, drag the arrow to the left. This shortens the clip. The cursor also changes to a double-headed arrow which means you can drag it back to its original length again. When you release the mouse button, as we do here at the 11 seconds mark, the clip is trimmed to that point. As always, keep an eye on the preview window to see the effect. When you trim a video clip, the corresponding audio track is trimmed accordingly.

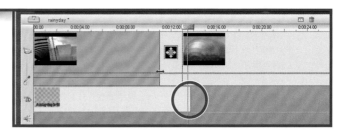

However, note that something rather odd has happened to the crawling caption in the example. When we shortened the clip to 11 seconds above, the caption in the overlay track was automatically trimmed as well. By default, captions are linked to video clips. It started off as a 26 second caption but has now been reduced to 14 seconds. Rather than dropping text from the caption, which would of course be daft, Studio simply speeds it up during playback. The problem is that text is now liable to fly past far too quickly on screen.

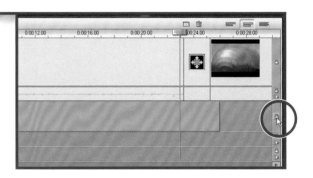

Let's say you want to keep the caption exactly as it was at the outset, regardless of any changes you make to individual clips. The way to achieve this is by 'locking' the title track before you trim the clip. The lock buttons – every track has one – are located at the extreme right-hand side of the Timeline. In this screenshot, we have restored the video clip to its original duration and we can see that the caption runs for 26 seconds again. We can now click the padlock icon for that track to lock it in place.

The titles track becomes shaded in grey to indicate that it is locked. We can now select and trim the clip as before without affecting the crawling caption. Here, we've trimmed it to 11 seconds again but the caption remains at 26 seconds. Click the padlock icon in the title track once more to unlock it.

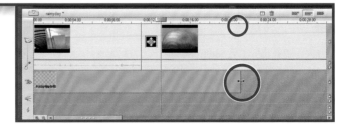

Let's now imagine that we've decided to speed up the caption by, say, five seconds to reduce the overlap with the second clip. Just as you trimmed the video clip, latch on the far right edge of the caption and drag it to the left to the tune of five seconds. We'll drop it at around the 21 second mark. The important thing here is that you can edit the overlay track quite independently of the video and original audio tracks. It's only when you edit the video track that other tracks follow suit unless you lock them first.

In this screenshot, we've dragged the caption to the right along the overlay track and dropped it in a new position. This again is something that you just can't do in Storyboard mode. It's also the way to add a crawling or rolling caption to a still image slideshow, something that we had difficulty with back on p83.

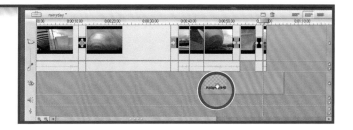

Finally for now, just to illustrate that you can edit video just as easily in the Timeline as in the Storyboard, select any clip. Use the timecode slider (or the transport controls in the preview window, or both) to find a suitable point for a break. With the video paused at the appropriate frame, click the split clip button on the toolbar. Just as in Step 5 on p68, the clip is split into two consecutive clips that can be treated independently.

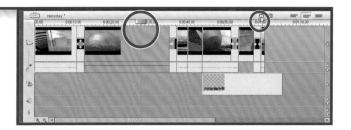

The split made, we can now right-click either clip and select Clip Properties for further trimming or to apply video effects or the Title Editor (should we wish to apply a caption). Or, of course, we could change the order of the clips, stick a still image between them, delete one or other or both, or move them around the project.

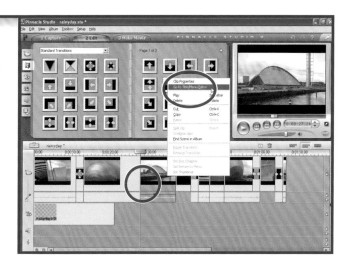

Finally, just a reminder to save your project as you go along. In Timeline mode, you are likely to produce fine edits that would take much longer to redo in the event of a program crash than simply shuffling clips around on the Storyboard.

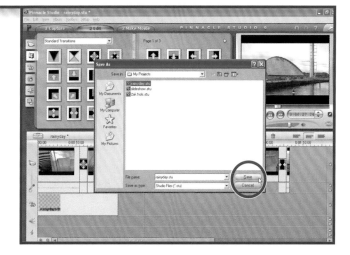

PART 5

Timeline tricks of the trade

Progressing from one clip to another with hard cuts or scene transitions is how movies are made. But if you watch pretty much any TV show or Hollywood movie, you'll notice that there's rather more going on than first meets the eye (or ear). Forget video effects – only for now, though, for we'll look at them in detail on p100-111 – and think a little more about transitions.

The L-cut

An L-cut is when the audio from one scene overlaps with the video in the next scene. Although the viewer may not consciously notice the effect, it can be remarkably effective. In this example, we have two consecutive scenes, one showing a downpour and the next a sunny beach. Our goal is to carry the sound of rainfall into the first few seconds of the beach scene.

An L-cut breaks the synchronisation between audio and video.

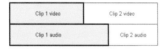

L-cut

Carrying the audio track from one clip through to the consecutive clip is an atmospheric and subtle way of making a scene transition.

1

First, some essential preparation. We're going to set up a three-second overlap so in clip 1 we must have three seconds of usable audio beyond the last video frame. Trim the clip so that its audio ends where you want it to, bearing in mind that you'll lose the final three seconds of the video footage when you make the L-cut. A relatively static shot of a puddle is perfect for this. Here we've trimmed the clip in the Timeline to ten seconds total.

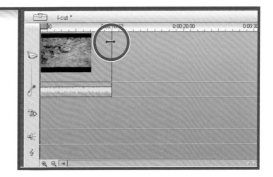

2

The second clip is even more important. As we'll see in Step 6, you need to have three seconds of good but hidden video footage at the start of the clip. Use the Clip Properties tool to trim the clip to the correct opening frame and then trim off a further three seconds. In other words, when you add the clip to the Timeline, the opening frame should actually be three seconds in from the frame that you really want to see. Confusing indeed, but bear with us…

3

The clips should be placed next to each other in the Timeline. We now need the soundtrack from the first clip to overlap with the video from the second clip. The way to achieve this is by shortening the video in the first clip while leaving the audio unchanged. First, lock the synchronised audio track by clicking the padlock icon at the far end of the Timeline. This track becomes greyed out to show that it can not be edited.

4

Now select the video clip and drag its right edge three seconds to the left to shorten it. Zoom in on the timecode to be precise. When you trim the video, the locked audio track remains unaltered.

5

What we have here is a three-second gap in the video track. Left unchanged, this would be a black screen in your movie. In fact, you can preview it if you like. The point is that during playback the pictures stop three seconds before the sound.

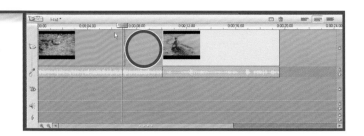

6

Now select the second video clip in the video track and drag its left edge three seconds to the left until it meets or very slightly overlaps the first clip. In effect, you're recovering the three seconds of footage trimmed in Step 2. Again, zoom in close for precision. The two video clips should now be adjacent with no gap between them.

Important note: do not drag the second video clip along the Timeline. The point is not to move it but merely to un-trim it.

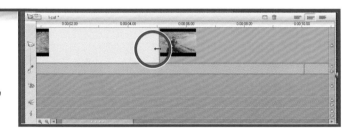

7

Zoomed out a little, we can now see the end result. In the first clip, the video ends three seconds earlier than the audio, producing the L shape that gives this effect its name. In the second clip, the video starts before the audio. The effect for the viewer is thus that the sound of rain carries on through to the sunny scene, making the transformation from puddle to beach all the more surprising. Unlock the audio track to complete the cut.

8

Here we have completed the effect by applying a scene transition between the clips. We have also split the second clip at the point where the sound from the first clip ends. This means we can fade out the sound of rainfall and fade in the beach sounds for a smooth audio transition. The overall effect (tricky to convey on paper) is thus:

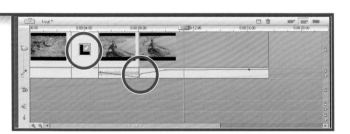

- *The sound of heavy rain and a close-up of a muddy puddle*

- *A gentle transition to a beach scene... but the sound of rainfall continues*

- *The rain dies away and the beach sounds come to the fore*

We talk about working with volume levels in the audio track on p112-114.

The J-cut

A J-cut is a transition in which video rather than audio overlaps from one clip to the next. It is performed in much the same way. Just a summary this time:

A J-cut is a kind of L-cut in reverse. This time, the video overlaps during the transition.

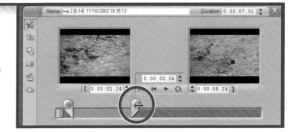

J-cut

This time, use Clip Properties to trim the first clip so that it is three seconds shorter than you want it to be for real. That is, trim the clip to the correct duration and then trim a further three seconds from the end (not the beginning).

Add the second clip to the Timeline next to the first clip. Now lock the audio track as before.

This time, un-trim the first video clip so that it overlaps the second clip by three seconds.

Finally, unlock the audio track. The second clip now has a J shape, hence the name. Again, we could continue with audio effects, split scenes, transitions, captions and so forth. At its simplest, though, the overall effect is:

- *The sound of heavy rain and a close-up of a muddy puddle*
- *Happy sounds of a beach… but still we're watching the rainfall*
- *The beach scene appears and links up with the soundtrack.*

Insert editing

In this example, we want to insert some still images in a video segment without interrupting the soundtrack. For instance, during the (by now familiar) beach scene, we would like to show some stills culled from a digital camera. But rather than having silence during the short slideshow, we want the sounds of the beach to continue in the background.

The principle is similar to the examples above but here we'll use the technique to take a break from and then return to a video clip. This would work equally well with an interview scenario when you have only one camera but want to show your own reactions as well as those of your subject. In the finished movie, you would cut away to a shot of yourself (presumably looking earnest) while the subject is talking then cut back to the subject. As the soundtrack is unbroken, the effect is seamless – and can be seen every evening on the TV news.

First of all, prepare your still images, slideshow or video that you want to use as an insert in the Storyboard or, preferably, the Timeline. Above all, note the clip's duration. If you're working with an image, set the duration in Clip Properties; if working with a video clip, trim it to the appropriate length. Here we have a sequence of five photographs with a ripple transition between them. The overall duration of the slideshow is 20 seconds.

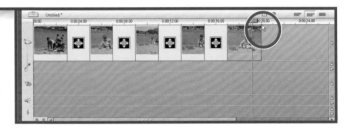

What we need now is a video clip into which we can insert this slideshow. The ideal candidate is one in which the soundtrack is undramatic but atmospheric. Place it on the Timeline next to the insert clip.

Lock the audio track now by clicking the padlock button. Now preview the second clip, decide where you want to insert the slideshow, and pause playback at that point.

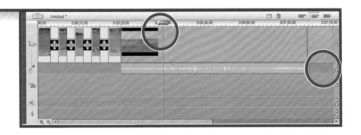

Split the clip here and then split it again twenty seconds further on. We now have three clips. Select the twenty-second middle section and delete it.

5

Note that the underlying audio track continues unbroken. We now have a 20 second black hole in our video track. That, of course, is just what we need.

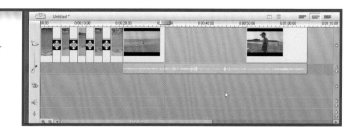

6

Select the entire slideshow by holding down the Control key while clicking on each image and transition in turn (or select your still image or video clip if that's what you're working with).

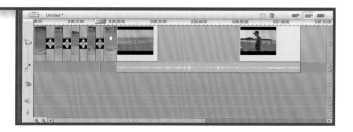

7

Now drag it along the Timeline and drop it into the gap vacated by the deleted segment of video. You should now have a seamless project in which live video changes to a slideshow and back again while the video soundtrack continues unabated.

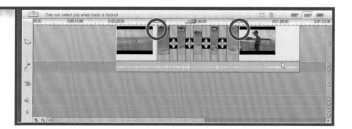

8

If you goofed on the measurements and your insert clip is too long or too short for the gap, either trim or un-trim it to fit or repeat Step 4 and delete the appropriate length of video. Unlock the audio soundtrack when you're finished.

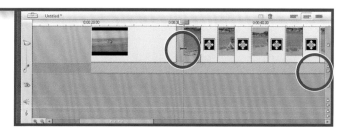

9

If you use a video clip as your insert, you'll find that its soundtrack gets left behind on the Timeline during the move. This is just what you want. When you unlock the audio track after the insertion, simply delete the redundant audio segment.

6

PART

DIGITAL VIDEO MANUAL

Doing more with your movies

PART 6

Video effects

Virtually all video editing software lets you capture footage from a camcorder, work in both Storyboard and Timeline modes, trim clips for length and apply basic enhancements like captions and transitions. But what if your raw footage is in no fit state to be seen? What if you forgot to set the white balance on your camcorder and a key clip is tinged with blue or red? What if a touch of camera shake mars an otherwise special shot? Or what if you'd like to transform your video into something altogether more interesting?

This is where video effects come into play. With the likes of Pinnacle Studio and Ulead VideoStudio, you can take any individual clip, sequence of clips or the movie project as a whole and apply special effects. These come under three broad categories:

- **Enhancement** Effects that help you repair flaws in the source footage, such as poor lighting and distorted colours
- **Fun** Effects that add a different feel and look to footage, such as turning a sequence sepia or running a clip in slow motion
- **Advanced** By which we mean video effects like transparent overlays and picture-in-picture

We'll run through some examples but the truth is that you need to experiment with your own footage and see what suits and what doesn't. Just as with fancy scene transitions and titles, it's easy to muck up a movie with overexuberance.

Repair and recovery
We'll look first at Studio's repair tools. Don't expect miracles – improving a video clip is a lot harder than enhancing a still image – but don't assume that flawed footage need necessarily be consigned to the cutting room floor.

1 *Open Studio in either Storyboard or Timeline mode and select the clip that you want to work with. To get things going, here we have a clip in which the camcorder's white balance was way off. The result is an unnatural blue tinge to the clip. Open Clip Properties and click the bottom tab to the left to get to the Video Effects controls.*

2 *There are five main options here – Cleaning Effects, Style Effects, Fun Effects, Color Effects and Time Effects – and each contains several sub-menus. We'll start by selecting the Auto Color Correct entry under Cleaning Effects. Click OK.*

3 *Hmm. The 'advanced' controls here amount to a brightness slider. Slide it to the right and the clip gets brighter; slide it to the left and the clip gets darker. Either way, it still looks blue. However, we can lighten it slightly to compensate in part for the overcast filming conditions. Click Add New Effect to return to the main menu.*

4 *Select Color Effects to see the sub-menu. One easy option would be to make the clip black and white or sepia, as shown here. This doesn't so much repair the poor white balance as completely mask it. However, without careful planning, a random sepia clip in the middle of a project simply looks odd.*

5 *Instead, we have selected Color Correction and clicked OK. This option provides four sliders that among them can alter the colours in the clip quite dramatically. With a little (OK, a lot) of trial and error, you should be able to reach a balance that makes your clip look more lifelike.*

6 *A panel to the left in the Video Effects screen lists which effects have been applied to the current clip. It's perfectly possible to overlay one effect on another, as indeed we have done. To remove an effect, select it in this panel and click the trash can icon.*

Always play the entire clip in the preview window to ascertain that your effects look good throughout. Remember that you can always trim a clip to preserve only the essential bits.

Some of the effects Studio provides are flagged with a padlock and a plus sign. You can experiment with them but if you want to lose the Pinnacle Systems watermark you'll have to pay up. Close the Video Effects window when you're finished and your chosen effects will be applied to the clip.

Camera shake is the bane of any amateur movie-maker's life. A tripod, monopod or brick wall can help you take steady shots but sometimes a little wobble is unavoidable. As discussed earlier, your camcorder may well have its own image stabilisation feature, but your video editor probably has one too. Trouble is, they don't work by magic so don't set your expectations too high. We find that Studio's implementation works reasonably well where movement is minimal. It's a one-hit effect with no fine-tuning controls.

Noise is a somewhat odd term used to describe interference on a video clip. Think of a snowy TV screen or an ancient film and you'll have the idea. Studio can reduce noise, but you'll find this more beneficial when working with digitised versions of old analogue recordings, such as a VHS video that you've transferred to your computer. The Motion Threshold button determines the level at which Studio applies noise reduction on the basis that trying to enhance a portion of video in which there is a lot of onscreen movement does more harm than good. The default setting is probably about right, but to be honest we've never had a great deal of success with this tool.

Jazzing it up in Studio

One of the most effective techniques you can apply to a clip is altering its speed. You might slow a segment down to focus the viewer's attention on a detail, perhaps adding a caption or narrated comment for extra emphasis or clarification, or speed a clip for comic effect.

Here's how to do it in Studio:

1

Select the clip in the Storyboard or Timeline and open Clip Properties. Now open the Video Effects screen. Click Time Effects in the main menu, then select Speed and click OK.

2

The presets – half-speed and double-speed – may be all you need here but it's possible to determine the speed manually. Click in the speed field and delete the current setting, then enter a figure of between 0.20 (one-fifth speed) to 10.0 (ten-speed). Hit OK to exit the field, and preview the effect in the preview window. The optional Smooth Motion checkbox reduces choppiness in slow motion effects.

3

Something rather obvious, but still worth mentioning, is that changing a clip's playback speed alters its duration. For instance, a 10-second clip played at half-speed becomes a 20-second clip. Note too that when the Video Effects box is open and Speed is selected, as shown here, you can speed up/slow down a clip directly on the Timeline. The mouse cursor becomes a clock with double arrows: use this to drag the clip to the right to extend its duration (i.e. slow down playback) and to the left to make it shorter (i.e. speed it up).

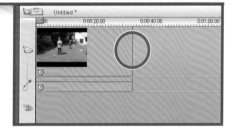

4

Elsewhere, Studio's Fun, Color and Style effects can be used individually or together to create all manner of wonders. Again, many of the better effects are provided on a pay-to-unlock basis. Here's the same clip edited with stained glass, mosaic, water drop, 'posterise' and added sunlight effects.

Key frames in VideoStudio

Ulead VideoStudio uses the concept of video 'filters' rather than effects, though it amounts to much the same thing. The program also comes stacked with many more options than Studio and the configuration options are extensive.

Perhaps more importantly, VideoStudio also offers key frame control over effects. This lets you customise the appearance of an effect throughout the duration of a clip, whereas with Studio an effect is all or nothing and follows a pre-determined path through the clip.

Here's a worked example.

We have a short clip in the Timeline that includes a zoom shot of an island. For reasons best known to ourselves, we'd like to overlay some bubbles on this clip, with maximum bubble density coinciding with maximum zoom. One way to achieve this would be to split the clip into three and apply the effect three times: a few bubbles during the opening and closing segments and a lot of bubbles in the middle segment. The other is to set key frames.

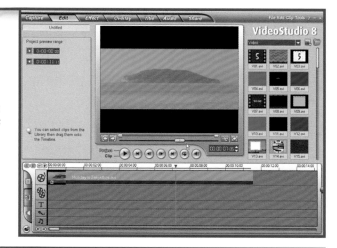

First we must add the effect. We've opened the Video Filter menu top right and dragged the bubbles filter onto the clip in the Timeline.

Bubble size, colour, frequency and so forth can be adjusted using one of the presets or the Customize Filter button. However, the same number of bubbles will be apparent throughout the whole clip. That's not what we want.

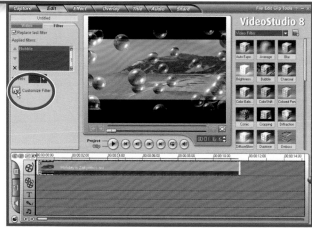

4

The trick now – and it's a tricky one – is to set the first key frame. Click the Customize Filter button and note the two preview windows. The one to the left, labelled Original, is the one to work with. Click the tiny Play arrow and the clip will play in the window. In the preview window to the right, you can watch the filter effect. Here we see bubbles, as expected. The effect will be uniform throughout the clip. Click Play again to pause playback.

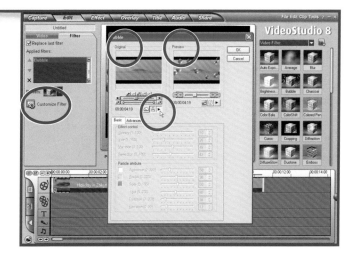

5

Now drag the slider in the Original window to the far left to return to the start of the clip. Use the Play control or the slider to advance to the beginning of the segment in which you want more bubbles to appear. Here it's just as the island comes into view.

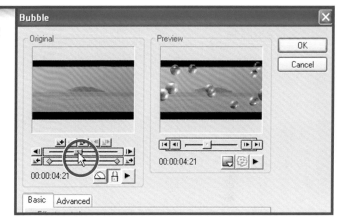

6

Click the miniscule Add Key Frame button above and to the left of the slider track. A red diamond appears on the lower key frame track. This is your first point of reference for tweaking the effect. Now use the slider (or Play control) to move to the end of the target sequence. Pause, and add another key frame.

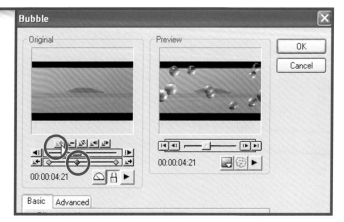

7

You should now have four key frames, including the default key frames at the very beginning and end of the clip. These effectively divide the clip into three sections. It's just like splitting the scene, in fact, only without actually making any cuts.

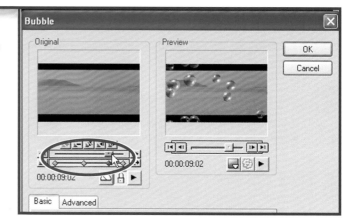

8

Click the first key frame – i.e. the one at the very beginning of the clip – to select it. The diamond turns red. Now adjust the filter controls for that key frame in the main panel, previewing the effect in the preview window as you do so. To keep things simple, here we'll reduce the bubble density figure to 5.

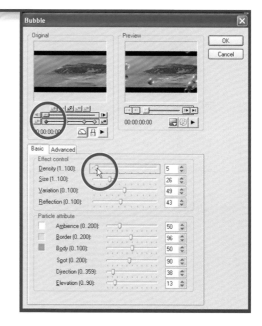

9

Now select the second key frame – i.e. the one that marks the start of your central segment – and adjust the filter controls once more. In this screenshot we've upped the bubble density to 25. Extra bubbles appear in the preview window so you can gauge the effect.

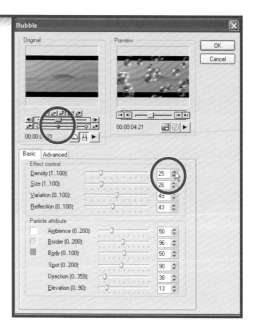

Now move to the third key frame – i.e. the one that marks the end of your central segment – and complete the tweak. We'll set the density level to 15 here. Five bubbles will thus be on screen when the clip begins, increasing to 25 and then reducing to 15 as the scene draws to a close. That's the theory, anyway...

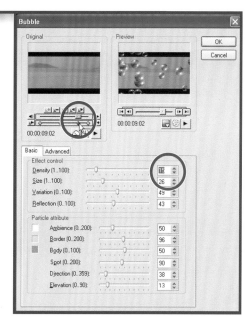

Click the Play button in the preview window to watch the effect in its entirety. If anything needs alternation, return to the key frames and fine-tune the effect further. VideoStudio blends the transition from one key frame to the next smoothly by default, so you get a gradual build up of bubbles from 5 to 25 rather than a sudden shower.

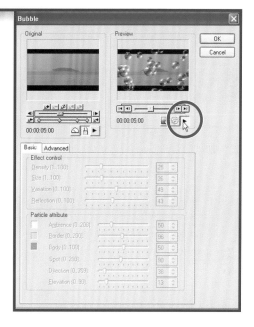

To see the effect for real, click OK and return to the main VideoStudio interface. Select the clip in the Timeline and play it through from start to finish. It's worth pointing out that VideoStudio sometimes struggles to render complex filters until you produce (save) the movie for real, but the preview window gives you a good idea of how it will turn out.

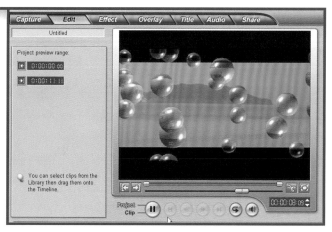

Transparent overlays

Let's say that you want to add a comedy shark fin to a clip of the sea. Bearing in mind how we worked with transparent title overlays back on p74-77, it should be obvious that the way to achieve this is with a transparent image placed in the overlay track of the Timeline. Trouble is, Studio doesn't provide any drawing tools as such beyond a few preset shapes and text tools. What we need is a separate image that we can overlay on the clip. Three things are required:

● Studio automatically makes one colour transparent when you overlay an image. Which colour is dictated by the top left pixel in the picture. This is so far from being obvious and intuitive that it's not funny, but there you have it. The

key to creating a transparent image of a shark fin is thus to draw the fin in on a solid background that can be completely erased. The greater the contrast between your drawing and the background, the better. We want a black fin, so we'll work on a white background.

● The image to be overlaid should be the correct dimensions for the video clip. In a PAL 4:3 clip, this means 768 x 576 pixels (as seen in Step 4 on p79 when we grabbed a frame from a video).

● The overlay should also match the clip. There's not much point overlaying a shark's fin if it ends up floating above the horizon. The easiest way to ensure a match is to grab a frame from the relevant clip and use this as your starting point.

Grab a suitable frame from the target video clip (see p79) and save it on your computer. Now open this image in your usual image editor. We'll be working with Paint Shop Pro.

Here is the grabbed frame. Because it was grabbed from the project, it is already the correct size for re-insertion.

Create a new image with the same dimensions as the grabbed frame – 768 x 576 pixels here – and a solid background colour. We've gone with white.

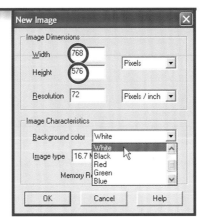

Draw your shark fin, or whatever. Yes, this is indeed an atrocious attempt but it makes the point all the same. We have the grabbed frame and the new blank canvas side by side to give us an idea of positioning. You could be clever and work with layers for proper control.

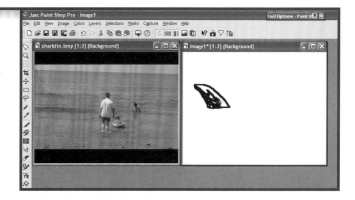

Save your drawing as a bitmapped image (extension BMP) and return to Studio. Make sure that the relevant video clip is visible in the Timeline. Now open the still images tab of the Album and navigate to your picture. Drag it into the overlay track on the Timeline.

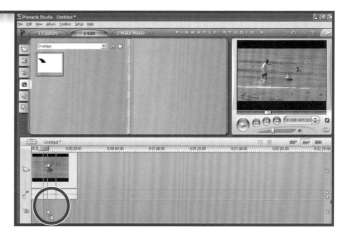

The finished article, more or less. The shark fin is superimposed on the video and the white background is completely transparent. Adjust the duration of the image to suit the clip.

Because the image is an element in the overlay track, you can edit it in the Title Editor. Double-click it in the Timeline to go straight there, and perhaps add a caption. Captions tend to reintroduce background shading, as shown here.

Picture-in-picture

What should be clear is that superimposing a still image on a video clip in Studio is neither straightforward nor particularly effective unless you take a very great deal of care (as we, patently, did not). Nor is it possible to add a video clip to the overlay track in Studio, so you can't run one clip over another. In VideoStudio, however, you can do this. The most useful outcome is a picture-in-picture effect. We'll look at that now.

For a change, our starting point here is a finished video produced in Muvee (see Appendix 3) replete with an acid colouration effect. We have imported this into VideoStudio. To one segment of the video we wish to add a 'talking head', but we don't want to cut away to a different scene. Rather, we want the subject to appear in a window during playback. In fact, we'll go further and make the window fade in and fade out. Sounds complicated? Not a bit of it.

Our main clip is in the Timeline and now we have to find the overlay clip. As always in VideoStudio, you navigate to saved media files in a panel to the right.

Preview the overlay clip in the main window by selecting it in the Album. If necessary, trim it for length with the in/out markers. When the clip is ready, drag and drop it into the overlay track just below the main video track.

Note the controls in the preview window. If you click Clip, only the clip that's currently selected in the Timeline plays; if you select Project, both clips play. The latter is what you want here. Drag the Timeline handle back to some point before the beginning of the overlay clip, and play the project. The second clip now appears in a window on top of the original clip. Drag the overlay clip along the Timeline until it kicks in at just the right point.

Now click on the overlay clip to select it. This opens up an Edit panel to the left of the preview window. Here you can mute the volume of the overlay clip, or have it fade in or out or both. If not muted, the overlay soundtrack will be mixed with the original audio during playback. You can also adjust the playback speed of this clip in isolation. To see the effect of a change, be sure to click the Project button in the preview window and drag the timeline marker back to the start of the overlap between the two tracks.

5

Next, click the Motion & Filter tab to open up further options. Here you can drag the overlay clip to any part of the frame, resize it, apply a little or a lot of transparency, and add a border. You can even apply filters to the overlay clip just as you can to a clip in the main video track (see p101). It's all really very clever.

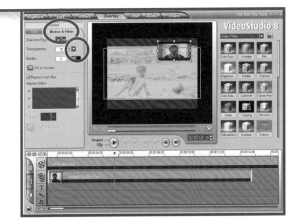

6

Note the Direction/Style button that determines whether the picture-in-picture is static or drifts across the screen from side to side or from top to bottom, and whether it fades in or out or both. Cleverer still.

7

Finally, click Project again, rewind, and preview the result. Here our talking head fades in and out of a bordered, static, semi-transparent window in the top right corner of the frame.

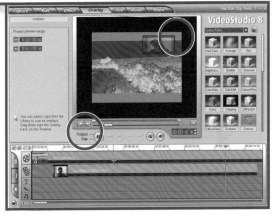

8

Such effects take a while to render in preview mode, so be patient. Also be very, very sure to save your project as you go along. Nothing crashes a program like picture-in-picture action.

DOING MORE WITH YOUR MOVIES

Working with audio

So far, we have largely ignored the role of audio in movie-making. However, there's a great deal you can do with sound, both to edit and enhance the original soundtrack and to add extra bells and whistles (perhaps literally). In particular, we're talking about background music, voice-overs and sound effects. In the following series of short workshops, we'll tackle the most common tasks.

Editing the original soundtrack

Our goal here is twofold: to remove a portion of the original soundtrack in part of the project and to adjust the volume in another. Here again we are working with Pinnacle Studio. In this example, the cameraman coughed during a clip that we don't want to ditch.

Switch to Timeline mode if you're not in it already and select the clip in question. The soundtrack is represented in the original audio track as a graphical waveform. The higher the peak, the louder the sound. The cough is the segment of high waveform activity just to the right of the Timeline marker i.e. from around 5.75 seconds to 6.5 seconds. Let's remove the cough completely.

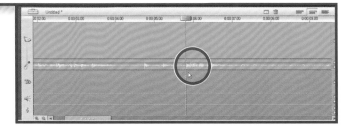

To edit the soundtrack without affecting the video track, we must undo their natural synchronisation. Earlier (p93), we locked the soundtrack to edit the video independently. This time around, lock the video track by clicking the padlock icon. It becomes greyed out.

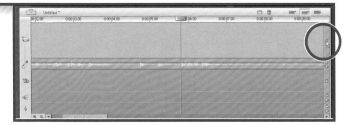

Using the Timeline marker as a guide, use the scene split button to make a cut immediately before and immediately after the cough. Play the clip in the preview window to check that you've isolated it precisely.

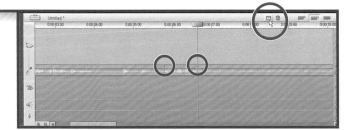

This isolated section of the soundtrack can now be selected independently and deleted. When you unlock the video track, the gap in the soundtrack remains and the cough is gone. Unfortunately, you also lose any ambient background noise, and the sudden silence in the movie may be just as jarring for the viewer as the cough.

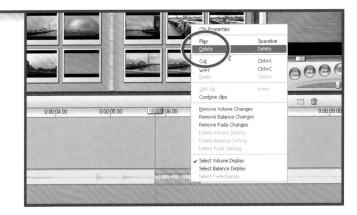

As an alternative to editing directly on the Timeline, you can use the Clip Properties box. With the video track locked, double-click the original audio track (or right-click it and select Clip Properties). However, this is more useful for trimming audio from the beginning or end of a clip (as with video) than for isolating and removing a mid-section.

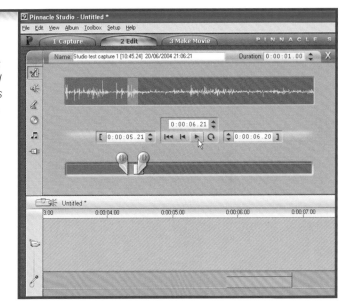

Back on the Timeline, let's try a different approach. This time it's not necessary to lock the video track. Select the clip with the cough and zoom in. Now note the level blue line running through the original audio track. This represents the volume level. When you point at the line, the mouse cursor changes to a blue speaker.

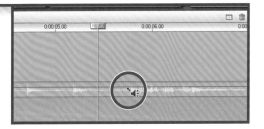

Click on the line about half a second before the cough – i.e. to the left of the first major peak – and keep the mouse button depressed. Now drag the cursor fractionally to the left or right. Release the mouse button, and you'll find that the line has grown a blue square. This is called a 'handle'.

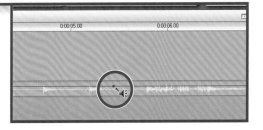

8

Repeat this procedure at the very beginning of the cough waveform, then again at the end of the cough, then once more about half a second further on. You should end up with four handles on the blue volume line.

9

Now click on the second handle and drag it downwards, towards but not quite to the bottom of the track. Repeat with the third handle. The idea is to reduce the volume of the cough. The purpose of handles 1 and 4 is to make this a smooth fade in and fade out rather than an abrupt cut to silence.

10

When you click on handles, the cursor changes to a highlighted speaker. In this mode, you can drag handles to the left and right as well as up and down. You might, for instance, want to drag the first handle to the left to increase the duration of the fade.

11

Preview the results continuously in the preview window by dragging the Timeline marker to the start of the effect and playing the clip in the preview window. Adjust the handles as often as necessary. The idea is to fade the cough sufficiently to make it less intrusive without killing the soundtrack completely. To complete the edit, you could also overlay a sound effect (see p122).

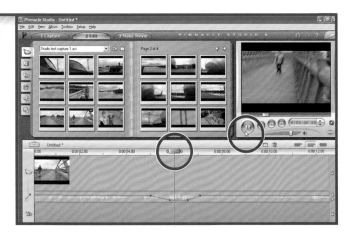

12

If you need to remove a handle, right-click it and select Delete Volume Setting. If you want to remove them all and start again, right-click anywhere on the volume line and select Remove Volume Changes.

Background music

As we saw when we first looked at the Timeline, Studio provides two additional soundtracks over and above the original audio track. The first that we'll look at is the background music track. It's worth noting, incidentally, that the audio track distinctions are purely arbitrary from a technical perspective. That is, you can as easily put an MP3 song on the narration/sound effects track as on the music track. However, we'll follow the convention here.

Do be aware that copying tracks from a commercial CD for use in a movie – or for any other use – is technically an infringement of copyright. However, it's highly unlikely that anybody will much mind so long as you don't show the movie to a public audience or post it on the internet for general dissemination. Gathering friends and family around the living-room television for a private audience is just fine.

With a movie project open in the Timeline, click the Sound Effects tab in the Album and navigate to any folder that contains MP3 or WMA tracks. Select a track and click Open.

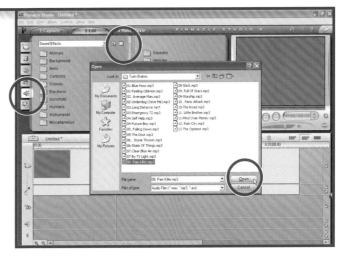

All tracks in that folder are now displayed in the Album. Drag one into the background music track in the Timeline. Here we can see that the track is longer than the video clip. Rather than have excess music at the end of the movie, we'll trim the audio to fit.

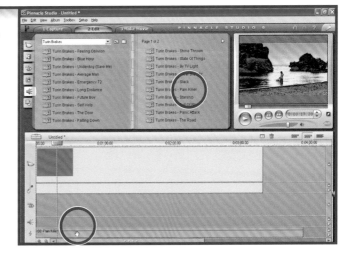

3

Right-click the track and select Clip Properties. The first time you do this, Studio analyses the file, but it only takes a few seconds. Now you can play the track in isolation in the Clip Properties screen.

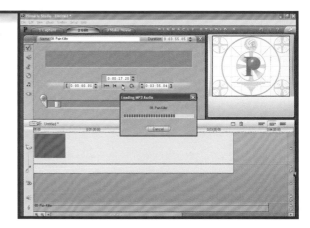

4

By positioning the Timeline marker at the end of the video clip, we can read the timecode in the preview window. Here the video clip lasts for about 3 minutes 20 seconds.

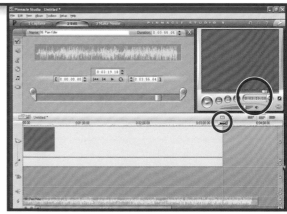

5

In the Clip Properties window, mark the cut-off point for the audio track at 3 minutes 18 seconds. This allows a couple of seconds silence at the end. Either use the sliding out-point marker or enter 0.03.18.00 in the out-point field, as shown here. Close Clip Properties when you're finished.

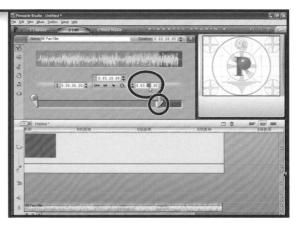

6

Back in the Timeline, the video and background music tracks are now more closely matched, with the music ending just before the video. However, because we clipped the track in its prime, it ends abruptly. You can tell this from the waveform without even previewing it.

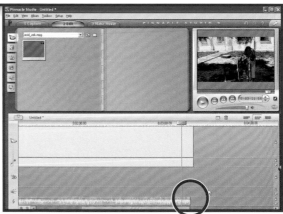

The answer, of course, is to fade out the track. As in the previous example, use handles on the blue volume line to control playback volume. Here we've gone for a gradual fade.

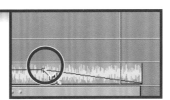

You might also want to temporarily reduce the volume – or kill it completely – at other parts in the project. If you want to remove a segment of music and leave a gap, select the track, split it into three sections and delete the middle section.

In this screenshot, we have used handles to reduce the volume at two strategic points in the project. You might do this if you're going to add narration or other sound effects, or perhaps just to bring the original sound to the fore. The point is that you can easily control the volume of the music throughout a clip or an entire project.

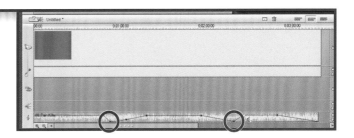

You can also edit an audio track directly in the Timeline just as you did with video. For instance, shorten an overlong track by latching onto its far right edge and dragging it left along the Timeline. This would save a trip to Clip Properties. You can also add new tracks, copy and paste clips from one point on the Timeline to another, and otherwise generate a complementary soundtrack that enhances your video.

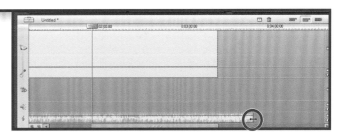

As one alternative to working with your own MP3/WMA music tracks, try Studio's SmartSound. Right-click anywhere in the background music track and select Generate Music. This opens a menu in the Album. Pick a style, a song and a version and preview it. Keep trying until you find something you like (not easy, we have to say).

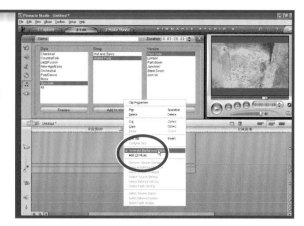

Now click Add To Movie and let Studio work its 'magic'. Shortly, you'll have a ready-made soundtrack that matches your project for length with no need for trimming. That said, you can edit the track in Clip Properties or in the Timeline just like any other.

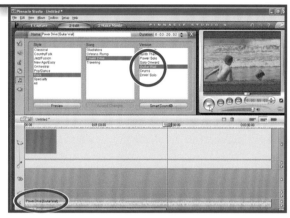

As another alternative, you might want to include a track from an audio CD in your movie project. One approach would be to copy, or 'rip', it separately and save it as a file on the hard disk (usually in WAV, MP3 or WMA format). But Studio lets you do this directly. Right-click the background music track, select Add CD Music and pop a CD in your CD or DVD drive.

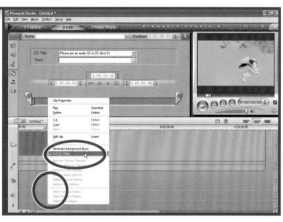

Tell Studio what the disc is called – its real title or anything else you fancy will do; next time around, Studio will re-identify it automatically – and click OK.

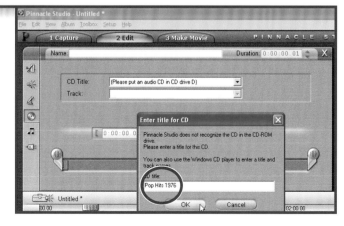

Now select the appropriate track number in the Track field and preview it to confirm that this is indeed the track you want. When you're sure, click Add To Movie.

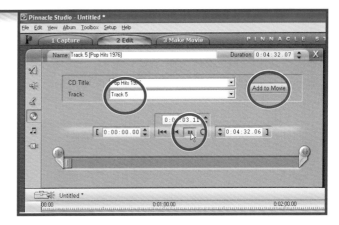

The CD track now appears in the background music in the Timeline. When you play the project for the first time, Studio 'extracts' the song from the CD. This done, you can hear it in the project and edit the track just like any other audio clip. You can also remove the CD from the drive now.

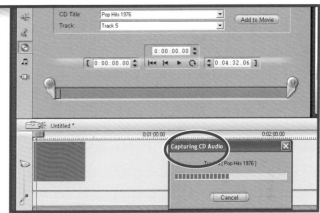

If this procedure doesn't work, click Setup on Studio's menu bar followed by CD and Voice-over. Here you can specify which drive Studio should look in for the disc – handy when you have two or more drives – and which extraction method it should use. The default is digital extraction, which will work with virtually any recent CD or DVD drive.

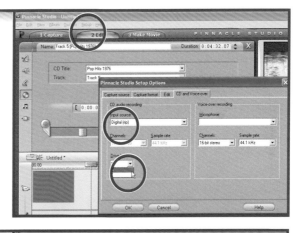

However, you can change this to an analogue extraction method if necessary. In this case, when you preview your project for the first time as in Step 16, Studio has to play the track through the sound card in order to record it. This is no problem but it takes considerably longer than a digital rip. Depending on your computer's sound card, you may also be able to record from an external device.

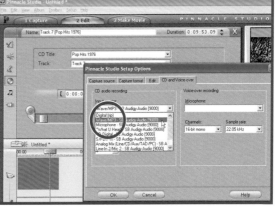

Narration

The sound effects track is intended to be shared with narration, which effectively means that you can't have a voice over at exactly the same point in a project as an effect. You probably wouldn't want to anyway. However, should this ever pose a problem, you could always drop either the effect or the narration into the background music track, assuming that there's no music already in place. The bottom line is that at any given time you can have two out of these three audio options:

- Sound effect
- Background music
- Narration

Plus, of course, the original video soundtrack.

By narration, we simply mean a recorded voice-over. Think of it as an alternative to enhancing the video with titles and captions. It's particularly useful for linking clips that otherwise might appear incongruous, or simply for telling a story from beginning to end. Slideshows particularly benefit from narration.

Indeed, you might even make narration the primary element in a project, in which case video, audio and stills serve to enhance the spoken word rather than vice versa.

Studio provides a tool specifically for recording your voice. As with sound effects, timing is everything: your words should synchronise with the pictures on screen. With this in mind, there are two main approaches to recording a voice-over. In the first instance, you would start recording at the beginning of a project and keep talking throughout, describing the pictures as they appear in real time. The key things here are a script and practice. Alternatively, you might prefer to record on a scene-by-scene basis, particularly if your voice-over will be used to punctuate the movie rather than provide a constant commentary. Either way, always remember that you can split a recording into smaller clips, trim them for length, and shuffle clips to precise points on the Timeline. If you miss a cue during recording, don't start again: just keep talking and then isolate and move the wayward portion during editing.

Connect a microphone to the mic jack of your computer's sound cards or, if it's a USB model, to a USB port. In Studio, click Setup then CD and Voice-over. This takes you back to the settings options we saw in Step 17 on p119. Select Microphone as the input source and set the quality levels. We recommend 16-bit mono/44.1KHz. Now, it should be as easy as this but you may have to configure your sound card's own software to activate the mic jack.

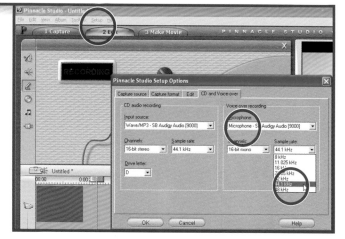

To start a recording, you must have at least one clip in the Timeline. If you intend to synchronise a recording with the movie in real time, you'll want to have the entire project in place. Right-click inside the narration track and select Record Voice-over. This opens the narration screen.

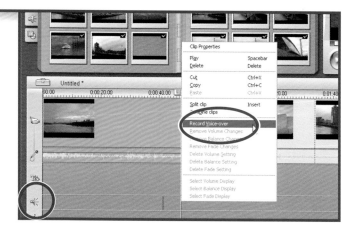

3

Talk into the microphone, monitor the volume level as you speak and adjust the slider as necessary so that the display stays mainly in the yellow zone, as here. Any higher, and you risk distortion; any lower, and you may not be heard.

4

Cue up your video a little before the point at which you wish to start recording, and play it in the preview window. If you need to hear the original audio soundtrack, keep the volume as low as you possibly can (or, better, wear headphones). The last thing you want is for the microphone to pick up the movie soundtrack during recording. Click Record, speak your piece, and click Stop when you're through.

5

Your narration now appears as an audio clip in the Timeline. As ever, you can trim, edit and reposition it. If you make a mistake, delete the clip and try again. Record as many segments as required to complete the project.

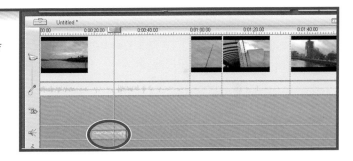

6

To hear a recorded clip in isolation from the original audio soundtrack, open it in Clip Properties and use the playback controls there (as opposed to the transport controls in the preview window). Save your project as you go along to preserve your recordings.

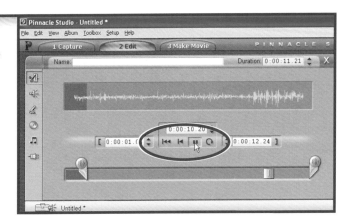

Sound effects

Nothing tricky here. The odd sound effect is great for bringing video to life by emphasising a point or raising a smile. For instance, wind howl brings atmospherics to a shot of a barren landscape, and tinned laughter or applause adds mirth to any pratfall. Timing is all, though, and we suggest leaving sound effects to the end of your project lest a last-minute scene transition or clip trim throws synchronisation out of kilter.

When you open the Sound Effects tab in the Album, the first thing you see is Studio's own collection of sound effects. If it's not immediately visible, select Sound Effects from the drop-down menu.

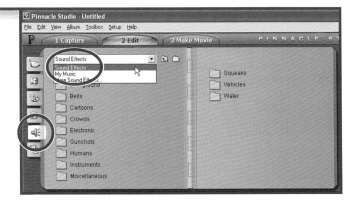

Studio's effects are themed and arranged in folders. Pick a theme and double-click it.

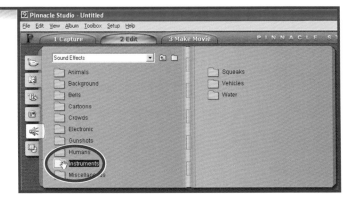

This opens up the relevant collection of effects. Click one to play it in the preview window. If you like what you hear, drag it to the sound effects/narration track in the Timeline.

To return to the theme menu, click the up-a-level arrow at the top of the Album's left-hand page. You can also use the folder icon to navigate to other sound effects if you have a collection saved on your computer (try searching the internet for samples and freebies).

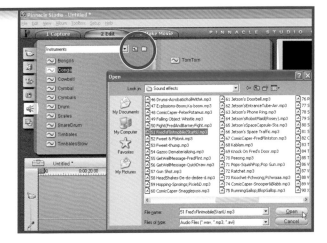

You know what's coming: any sound effect in the Timeline can be edited directly or opened in Clip Properties; can be trimmed, moved and copied; can have its volume reduced, increased, faded in and faded out or altered; and can otherwise be handled like any other audio clip.

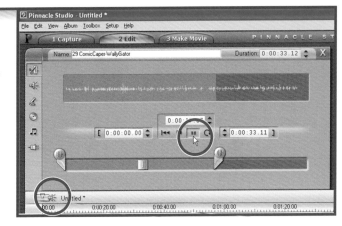

Audio effects

We looked at ways of enhancing video clips on p100-111. Well, Studio also lets you apply effects to audio clips. You might, for instance, want to apply a spooky reverb effect to your narration as the gondola passes under a bridge or the ghost passes through a wall.

If you want to edit the original soundtrack, lock the video track first. Otherwise, you can work with recorded narration, an imported sound effect or your background music. In this example, we have locked the video track and split the original audio track to isolate a very short sequence. We can now select this clip and open Clip Properties.

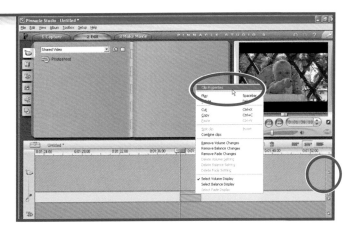

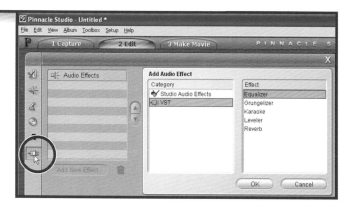

Click the Audio Effects tab to the left. Two menus appear: Studio Audio Effects, which offers a fairly sophisticated noise reduction tool; and VST, which offers five other options. Select one of these and click OK to get to the configuration screen.

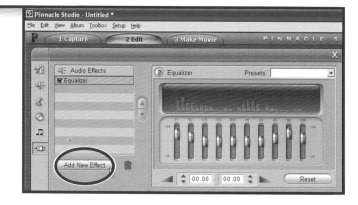

Here, for instance, we have the Equalizer. This lets you modify a clip's tone i.e. bass and treble. Note that whatever tweaks you apply affect only the clip that is currently selected in the Timeline. Close the Audio Effects window now or, as here, click Add New Effect.

This is the Reverb tool. It comes loaded with a selection of presets that provide more or less echo and 'hollowness'. These are highly effective but you can also fine-tune various settings. Use audio effects one at a time or combined. To ditch an effect, select it in the panel on the left and click the trash can icon.

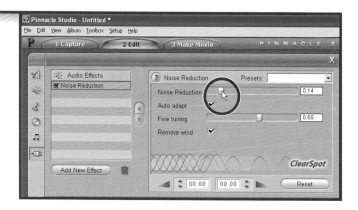

And so on and so forth. The Noise Reduction tool repays exploration, particularly if your original soundtrack is hampered with wind noise, hiss or crackle. The Leveler tool seeks to balance the volume level throughout a clip or project; Karaoke tries (and, in our experience, always fails) to remove the vocals from a song; and the Grungelizer crashes Studio. Your mileage may vary.

Mixing soundtracks: volume levels

It's entirely possible that your movie project will develop with four separate sound sources: the original audio recorded with the video footage, background music, voice-over narration, and sound effects. These soundtracks probably won't (and certainly shouldn't) run concurrently throughout. For instance, you may only use a sound effect once and your use of narration may be minimal or non-existent. However, the most important thing is to achieve a balance.

At one level, this is very easily achieved. We have already looked at how to alter the volume of any audio clip, be it a whizz-bang effect or a long MP3 track, with the blue volume control line that runs through the Timeline. If your background music is too loud in relation to your original audio, turn it down by dragging the entire volume line to a lower level (or use the Audio Toolbox: see Step 7 on p117).

Indeed, you can use handles to control the volume at every point in your project. The relative volume of each track in relation to the others is more important than the overall volume i.e. you can always turn your TV volume up or down during DVD playback but there's no cure for a voice-over that splits the eardrums or gets lost in the background music.

The key, then, is to preview your project with your ears as well as your eyes and adjust volume levels in the Timeline until you achieve aural perfection. We suggest that you use the original audio soundtrack as the baseline and edit the other tracks to fit in.

If you add a handle to the volume line in the audio track and then slide it all the way to the far left, you can alter the volume for the entire track in one movement just by dragging the volume line up and down.

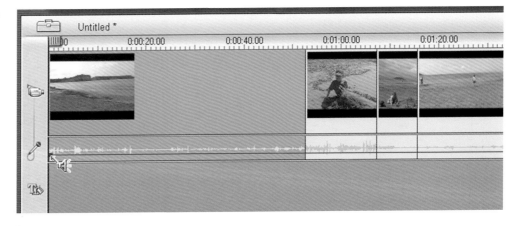

Mixing soundtracks: stereo balance

But there's more. Studio also allows you to adjust the stereo balance for each track. This means that you control whether a particular sound is heard from only the left speaker or only the right, or more from one than the other. You can also shift the balance throughout a clip.

Say you have a shot of a person walking from left to right across the screen, and the sound of their footsteps is clear. You could easily isolate this section of the audio track and adjust the stereo balance so that the footsteps play through the left speaker first, followed by both speakers, followed by the right speaker

alone. Get the timing right – i.e. tweak the stereo balance to match your pictures – and you'll add a different dimension to your movies.

If, incidentally, you're wondering whether it's worth it, find a short clip that's amenable to a stereo effect and produce two mini-movies: one without adjustment and one with. Then burn them to the same DVD or CD and play them in your DVD player. So long as your TV has stereo speakers, we reckon you'll be sold on the effect.

Adjusting the stereo balance is easy. Here's how.

Here we have some rather dull footage of a helicopter passing from right to left and getting closer. The idea is thus to fade the stereo balance from right to left to make the sound of its engine follow its motion. You can tell from the shape of the waveform that the volume also increases as the chopper gets closer.

Right-click the original audio track and click Select Balance Display. The track turns green with a black line running dead centre. It looks like the volume control but this line actually represents the stereo balance. Drag it up and the sound moves to the right speaker; drag it down and the sound moves to the left. If you were to position the line one-quarter of the way up from the bottom of the track, the sound would be three times stronger from the left speaker than the right.

Here we have faded the track gradually from right to left, using handles as before (see p113-114). The soundtrack is now stronger in the right channel at the outset, to match the helicopter's position, and moves with it (roughly) from right to left. At the very end of the track when the audio is loudest, we included a sudden dip to the extreme left channel. This coincides with the helicopter flying off screen.

Mixing soundtracks: surround sound

There's even more. If you have a 5.1 surround sound speaker system attached to your computer or your DVD player, you can also adjust the position of an audio track relative to the front and back speakers. For instance, in a shot of somebody walking towards and past the camera, you could fade their footsteps from the front speakers to the rear. The viewer will then hear the subject walking towards them, pass by, and continue walking out of sight behind them. You can use this effect in conjunction with the stereo balance to make footsteps (or anything else) move from left to right and from front to back, or any other combination. With the volume control, you can also make the volume of the footsteps fade in gradually as the subject approaches the camera, peak just as he passes by, and then fade away as he continues walking out of sight.

To enable surround sound editing, click Toolbox on the main program menu bar and select Change Volume. This opens the Audio Toolbox. In the top-right corner is a drop-down menu that tells Studio whether you wish to edit in stereo or surround sound. Unless Surround is selected here, you won't be able to open or edit the Fade view in your audio tracks. Now, it's quite possible that

A 5.1 surround sound system adds realism to movie playback.

your PC only has stereo speakers, or indeed that you use headphones, but you still want to produce a surround sound movie for playback on your DVD player's 5.1 sound system. In this case, select Surround. Just bear in mind that you won't be able to preview the effect of fade changes on your computer during editing, which means having to rely on educated guesswork.

1

This time around, right-click the audio soundtrack and click Select Fade Display. The track turns orange. The central black line now represents the balance between the front stereo speakers and the rear stereo speakers i.e. between the front and rear channels in a 4.1 or 5.1 sound system.

2

Drag the line up to shift the balance towards the front speakers and down to shift to the rear. Here, we have faded the sound of the chopper gradually from front to rear with a sharp drop-off at the end as it passes overhead.

3

As in the volume display, you can remove a handle by right-clicking it and selecting Delete Fade Setting; or remove all fade settings by right-clicking anywhere in the track and selecting Remove Fade Changes.

Mixing soundtracks: an alternative approach

If you find dragging lines around the Timeline something of a fuss, no matter: Studio offers an alternative graphical approach to audio mixing. You can achieve precisely the same results but you may find this way of working more intuitive.

1

Here we have a short project in the Timeline that includes the original audio in one track, background music in another, and a little narration and a sound effect sharing the third audio track. To select the entire project, click any clip to select it and use the Select All command on the Edit menu.

2

Now click the right-hand side of the toolbox icon. This is an alternative way to open the Audio Toolbox that saves going through the Toolbox menu. Click the loudspeaker option second from the top to open the screen shown here.

3

Again, note the drop-down menu top-right. You must select Surround here to enable the Fade controls, whether or not you actually have a surround-sound speaker system connected to your computer.

4 There are three sliders in this screen, one each for the original audio, narration/sound effects and background music tracks (in that order from left to right). In this screenshot, all three tracks are active (i.e. selected in the Timeline) and the graphical level meters show the volume level at the current point in the project during playback.

5 Let's say we want to reduce the background music volume for the duration of one clip. Play the project and pause right at the start of that clip. Drag the third slider downwards. This reduces the volume level for that track at that point. Use the Timeline marker to scroll forward until the end of the clip. Pause again and restore the slider to its original position. The result is shown here. Note the altered volume line in the music track (at the bottom), replete with handles. This is simply an alternative to editing volume in the Timeline directly.

6 With a little practice and a lot of previewing, you might find that you can adjust the volume of each track in real time during playback without having to pause for each tweak. Use a steady hand to achieve smooth fades. The moment you can do this successfully, add 'digital sound engineer' to your CV.

7 Above each slider are two buttons. The first mutes a track completely; the second adjusts the track's overall volume level. These are both one-hit controls that don't offer clip-by-clip control. For instance, if you want to make your background music track louder as a whole, click the knob and drag it clockwise; or if you want to kill it altogether, use the mute button.

Below the sliders are handy fade-in and fade-out controls. Move the Timeline marker to any point of the project and click the fade-in (left) button for one of the audio tracks. The volume will drop to zero at that precise point – it doesn't need to be the beginning of a clip – and then fade in over the course of two seconds, as shown here. The fade-out button does the opposite.

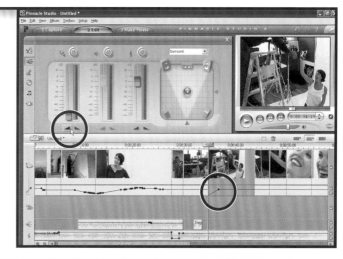

To the right of the volume faders are the balance controls. By default, all three tracks start life balanced centrally, represented by a straight line running through the middle of the Timeline track (as we saw on p112). However, here we have three icons representing the three tracks, and each can be dragged to the left or right to alter the position of the sound.

Like the volume controls, these edits can be performed in stages clip-by-clip or in real time throughout the length of a project. In this example, we are dragging the sound effects track towards the right channel or speaker. Changes affect the project in real time.

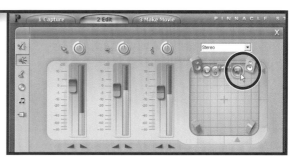

When Surround is selected, you have an additional option. The track icons can now be dragged to the front and back of the window to determine the balance of that track relative to the front and rear speakers in a surround sound system. Again, work in real time or in stages, whatever suits. To see the effect in the Timeline, you have to manually switch to Fade display (right-click a track and click Select Fade Display).

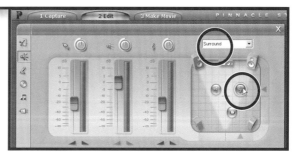

At any time, you can undo your edits one at a time via the Edit menu (click Edit > Undo) or by pressing the Control + Z keys simultaneously. To undo edited settings for an entire track in one move, right-click that track and select Remove Volume/Balance/Fade Changes as appropriate. This restores the default pre-edit track settings.

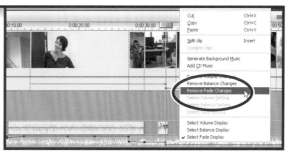

PART 7

Rendering, saving and sharing

The render agenda

When you compile a project with scenes, transitions, effects, titles and all the rest, it is important – nay, vital – to appreciate that you have not as yet made a movie. Indeed, your original source footage, whether video captured from a digital camcorder or a video file imported into the editor, remains intact and unchanged on your computer's hard drive. So far, your video editor has merely shown you how your project would look for real should you proceed to the next step. It's time for that next step now...

Catering for an audience

Before you can emerge with a finished movie, your video editor has to apply all those decisions, edits, tweaks, overlays, soundtracks and so forth to the source video. This process is called rendering and it's extremely demanding on your computer hardware. Obviously enough, the fancier your movie project, the longer it takes to render. Every custom transition between scenes, every caption and every effect, adds a few seconds or minutes to the process.

During rendering, an entirely new video file is created. This file is the movie proper: an edited and encoded version of your original footage. Again, though, your source video file remains intact on the hard drive and you can return to it time and time again to build new projects.

The format of your new file is a critical decision, and in fact one that you take before rendering begins. Your options are many and varied but all boil down to what you want to do with your movie and how you want to share it.

Rendering is a slow process. With long and complex projects, you'd be well advised to let your computer take the strain overnight.

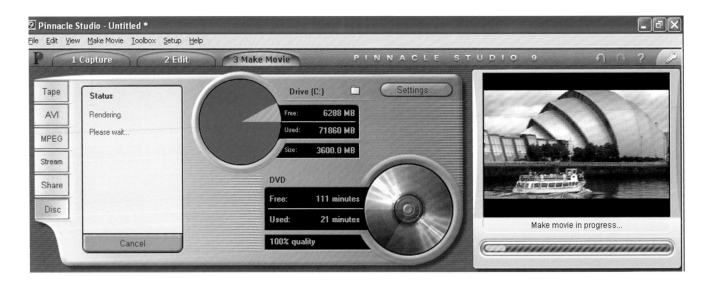

Playback on computer

This is the simplest of all possibilities: save your video as a file that you can play in Windows Media Player or another software player on your computer. You can also play it on any other computer so long as it has the same codec installed. A codec, if you remember, is a technology used to compress a video file.

Chances are the first time you view a rendered movie will be on your PC, but you'll soon want to progress to a wider audience.

Playback on the web/sharing via email

If you have some web space – and you probably do, as some is provided free as a matter of course by most Internet Service Providers – you can 'publish' your video file online. Anybody in the world with a web browser can then enter the appropriate URL – something like **www.yourdomain.com/holidayvideo.wmv** – and either save a copy of the file onto their own computer or 'stream' the video for live playback. In the latter case, a viewer can begin watching a 10MB video as soon as the first 30 seconds or so have been downloaded, and continue watching while the remainder of the file downloads in the background.

Once you have saved your video file on the hard disk, you'll have to upload it into the correct folder in your allocated slice of web space. This is the business of File Transfer Protocol, which simply means copying the file through the internet from your computer to another computer owned by your Internet Service Provider (or perhaps a web host, if you have your own domain). If this is all double Dutch, don't panic: check your ISP's website for help with FTP and web space. There's sure to be a step-by-step guide that steers you through program settings.

It may strike you as rather easier to email your video file to a recipient but the problem here is that email providers, including ISPs, restrict the size of file attachments. You may find that you can't send anything over 5MB without it bouncing. Posting your movie on the web is thus a useful approach when the video file is too large to email. Even here, though, you will be restricted by

the amount of web space available to you, and you should also bear in mind the time it takes to download at the other end. Only a very forgiving relative on the wrong end of a dialup modem will wait (and pay, in phone call charges) for a 50MB video file, no matter how impressive your movie.

The bottom line is that bandwidth restrictions force you to keep video files small when you want to share via the web or email.

With Studio 9, you get access to a free web-based account for sharing your videos. The available storage space is, er, a less than whopping 10MB.

With the VCD and SVCD formats, you can make movies that play in DVD players even if you don't have a DVD writer drive.

Playback on CD

Such concerns are irrelevant when you move up to a physical medium such as a recordable CD. Here you have three options:

- **Data disc** You can save a copy of any video in any file format onto a blank CD so long as it's under 700MB. This is no different in principle to copying a document onto a floppy disk and accessing it elsewhere.
- **Video CD** Secondly, and better, you can burn a Video CD (VCD). This is a special type of CD that stores the video file in a particular file format (MPEG-1) and in a particular folder structure that makes it readable to most DVD players. The quality level is akin to that of VHS video, with around one hour of video per disc.
- **Super Video CD** Finally, you can opt for Super Video CD (SVCD). This uses the same file format as DVD but with rather higher compression. You'll get 20–30 minutes of video on a single disc at near-DVD quality levels. Both VCDs and SVCDs can include DVD-style menus.

For a fourth option, see Appendix 2.

Blank recordable DVD media is cheap and hugely flexible.

Playback on DVD

But if you have a DVD writer, why not go the whole hog and make a 'proper' DVD? This way, you'll have a disc containing up to one hour of superb quality video that can be played in any DVD player. With menus and sub-menus, clickable buttons, chapter points for easy navigation and more, a home-made DVD can resemble a commercial Hollywood production in virtually every regard.

Many of the newer DVD writers now support dual-layer recordable DVDs, which effectively doubles your playback time. Double-sided discs are another, rather less attractive option where you put one movie on one side of the DVD and a second on the other side. Recordable media (i.e. blank discs) is getting cheaper by the day, as indeed are the drives, and the 'will it/won't it play on my DVD player?' compatibility issues of old are now on the wane. In short, just about every DVD writer will produce DVD movies that will play on just about all DVD players.

Of course, you can also save video files directly to blank DVD discs without bothering to 'author' a DVD movie project. In this way, you can transfer files of up to 4.7GB at a time from computer to computer. Just bear in mind that these simple data discs cannot be played in a DVD player (with one important exception: see p161).

Copying to tape

Rather than using the web, email, CD or DVD, you might want to copy your finished movie onto a VHS video tape for playback in a VCR, perhaps to give a copy to somebody who has neither a PC nor a DVD player. Such analogue tapes lack the resolution and quality of a digital medium and deteriorate with each play, but VHS is not quite dead yet.

The easiest approach is to copy your movie from your computer to your digital camcorder and from there to your VCR. Most video editors let you export a rendered movie directly to a digital camcorder via the FireWire connection, but only if your camcorder has a two-way socket (see p17). You can then hook up the camcorder's analogue output to the VCR's analogue input via an S-video or composite video cable connection, play the movie on the camcorder and re-record it with the VCR onto a blank VHS tape.

Some camcorders even feature a pass-through mode whereby you can connect the camcorder to the computer digitally via FireWire, hook it up simultaneously to a VCR, and record the movie directly to VHS tape without having to record it on the camcorder's MiniDV tape first (a kind of reversal of the analogue capture procedure described on p18).

If your camcorder doesn't have a two-way FireWire socket, you can use an analogue connection between the computer and camcorder. Some video capture cards support analogue output as well as input, but otherwise you'd need a separate breakout box or gizmo to provide the appropriate sockets and connections.

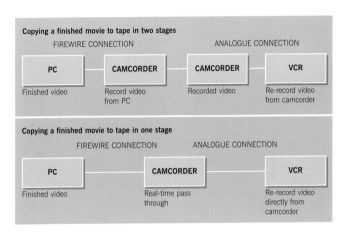

Re-recording to VHS tape with the camcorder as middleman.

File format choices

We discussed some of the many (many, many!) video file formats back on p28 and your video editor is going to offer you a bamboozling array of options and codecs when you come to render your movie. Rather than fill up the rest of this book with a pros and cons analysis, here's a quick summary of our recommendations.

- **For computer/web/email** Use Microsoft Windows Media Video (a WMV extension). This format offers a flexible range of quality versus file size configurations. WMV videos can also be played on all Windows PCs with the Windows Media Player program.

  An excellent alternative is the DivX codec, which we discuss in Appendix 2. However, you can only play a DivX movie on a computer that has the (free) DivX codec installed (see p161).

- **For CD/DVD** No real choices here. VCDs use the MPEG-1 file format and both SVCDs and DVDs use MPEG-2. However, within these restrictions, you can play around with the frame size and bit rate to tailor video quality levels. In this way, you might choose to reduce the overall quality a tad in order to squeeze a long movie onto a single disc.

- **For tape** Your video editor makes this a no-brainer by exporting the rendered movie in its native format without converting it to another file type first. If your project is based on footage captured from a digital camcorder, then it is kept in the DV AVI format.

PART

Saving your movie as a file

To save your movie as a file on the hard disk, you have a few straightforward choices to make. We'll look at these here, working again in Studio. Our starting point is a finished project that contains a soundtrack, sound effects, narration, scene transitions, captions and titles and all the other paraphernalia that goes into making movies.

Just a quick word first about saving unedited captured footage for backup and archival purposes, as mentioned on p59. In this case, you should add your entire footage to the Storyboard or Timeline in its raw state – i.e. without applying any edits whatsoever – and save it as a file. Pick the highest quality file format that you can, ideally MPEG-2. However, keep an eye on the estimated file size as you'll have to find a way of copying the results from your computer to (probably) CD or DVD. If you have a DVD writer drive, you can compress one hour of digital camcorder footage into an MPEG-2 file that will fit on a single disc. This way, you can re-record over your MiniDV tapes secure in the knowledge that you have a backup copy of the original footage. Keep the disc somewhere safe.

1

Click the Make Movie module tab. Studio now presents several options, including AVI, MPEG and Stream. We want to make a WMV file suitable for posting on a website. Click Stream and then Settings.

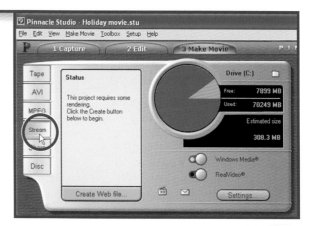

2

You can choose between the Windows Media and RealMedia file formats here. We recommend the former. Select it now and click the Settings button. Up pops a dialogue box.

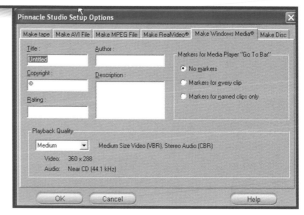

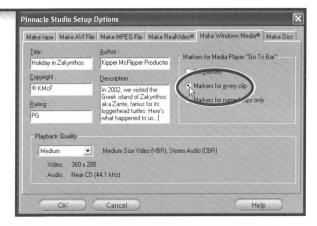

3

Information that you enter here will be visible to viewers when they play your movie in Windows Media Player. The markers section is optional but this lets your audience skip through the movie scene by scene.

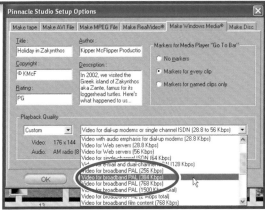

4

The critical bit. In the Playback Quality section, select one of the presets – Low, Medium or High – or select Custom and take your pick from this expansive menu. We've gone for one of the lower broadband options. This will produce a file that's suitable for watching over the internet through a broadband connection. If you're not happy with the final video, you can always return here and render the project at one of the other settings.

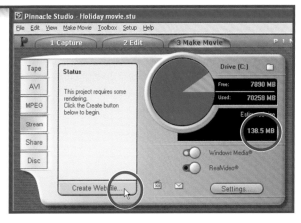

5

Click OK when you're through. Note that Studio now tells you – warns you, rather – that the project requires rendering. Note also the estimated file size. In this case, it's a whopping 135MB, which is far too large for the web. Ignoring that for a moment, click the big green Create Web file button.

6

Name your video file. By default, Studio uses the same title as your project. However, you can't have any spaces in the file name if the file is going to be published on the web so rename it now if necessary.

7

Studio now renders the movie and saves it as a file in the folder you selected in Step 6. This can take a very long time indeed, depending on the length and complexity of your project and the speed of your computer. Click Cancel if you change your mind.

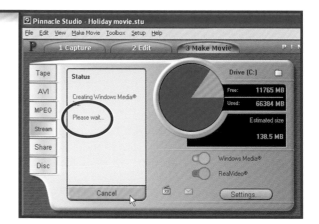

8

Returning to that file size now, what are your options? Well, the first would be to shorten your movie considerably by dropping scenes. This means reworking the entire editing process. The second would be to choose an alternative encoding quality. At the Low preset, for instance, the file size is reduced to a more manageable but still large 31MB.

9

The smallest file size that we could achieve in the WMV format was just under 7MB. However, if you haven't appreciated the trade-off between file size and video quality until now, you soon will. Our suggestion is that you experiment by isolating two short scenes linked with a transition and rendering them at different settings. See how low you can go without reducing video quality to an unacceptable level.

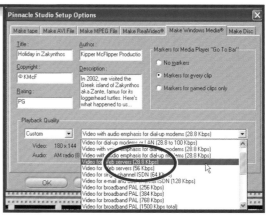

10

Here, for instance, we see a scene rendered as a small, and hence low-quality, WMV file. The frame size is small, resolution is abysmal and the audio is dreadful. The point is that a smaller, shorter movie rendered at a high quality is much more satisfying than a longer but unwatchable alternative. As a rule of thumb, 10–15MB is about as big as you'd want to go for a streaming web movie.

Let's now look at some alternatives. If you want to save your movies as an MPEG-1 or MPEG-2 file ready for burning to disc, select MPEG from the Make Movie menu. Once again, click Settings.

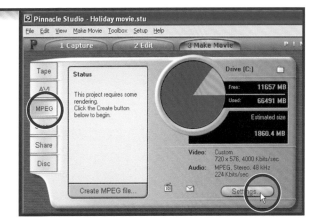

Studio offers several presets or templates, including instant compatibility with the VCD, SVCD and DVD formats. Select whichever is appropriate and the program will create a file that can be burned straight to disc without further encoding. Here, for example, we have selected DVD Compatible to produce an MPEG-2 video file with a frame size of 720 x 576.

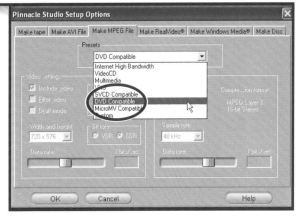

Back in the main screen, note the estimated file size. In this case, it's 2741MB which will fit comfortably on a 4.7GB DVD. However, let's say we wanted to fit two similar length movies on the same DVD. Return to the Settings menu and choose Custom.

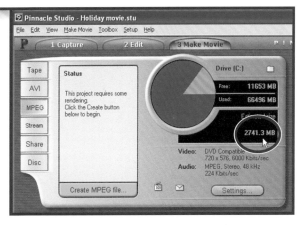

The beauty of MPEG-2 is that you can tailor it to suit. Swapping from constant bit rate (CBR) to variable bit rate (VBR) reduces the estimated file size by 250MB or so (see p142 for details of bit rates). However, as Studio can't know for sure how much space can be saved with VBR encoding until it actually does it, this is just a guess.

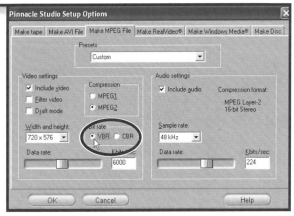

For a more dramatic reduction, try changing the bit rate from the default 6,000Kbps to 4,000Kbps. This shrinks the file size to 1,700MB. There will be a corresponding reduction in video quality but you can preview the result by encoding a scene or two.

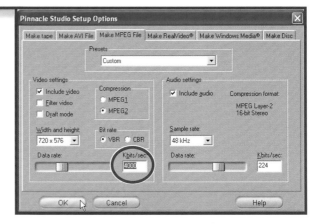

Conversely, you might like to push the bit rate up to 8,000Kbps or beyond if you have room to spare on your DVD. This preserves even more of the native DV AVI quality. At 10,000Kbps VBR, our project would weigh in at an estimated 4,134MB, which is just right for a DVD. Pushed to the 12,000Kbps VBR limit, though, it would require over 4,900MB and thus be too large for a single disc.

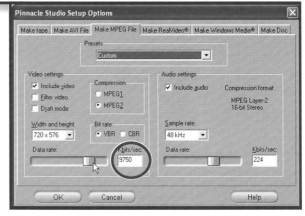

Importantly, while you can also tweak the settings for MPEG-1 video, you won't be able to make a Video CD if you stray from the strict VCD template (i.e. 352 x 288 frame size with a 1,150Kbps constant bit rate). This won't matter if you want to play your movie back on your computer using Windows Media Player or similar, but stick with the template if you want to burn a disc.

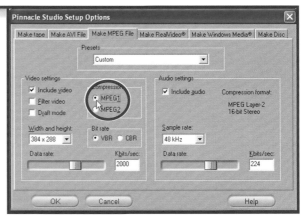

You can also render your movie in its native DV AVI format (assuming that you're working with footage captured from a digital camcorder). To do this, move to the AVI section and look for the appropriate codec in the Compression menu. In Studio, this appears as DV Video. Alternatively, just click the Same as Project button. The file size, incidentally, will be over 12GB. See Appendix 1 for details of why you might want to do this.

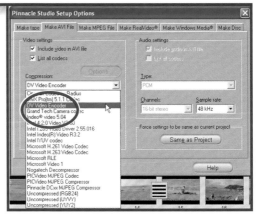

PART

Saving your movie to tape

Our purpose here is to render a project in Studio and then export it directly to a digital camcorder. We could then connect the camcorder to a TV, to enjoy the movie on the big screen, or to a VCR, to copy the movie onto VHS tape, or just lock the MiniDV tape away for safe-keeping.

Note that this is only possible if your camcorder has an enabled digital input i.e. a two-way FireWire port.

1

Connect the camcorder to the computer via a FireWire cable in the normal manner. Pop in a new tape and set the camcorder to VCR/playback mode (and not, as you might expect, camera/record mode). In Studio, with your project open, click the Tape tab. Now open the Settings menu and check the box that allows the program to control the camcorder. Ensure that DV Camcorder is selected in the Playback devices field. Leave the Record delay time at the default.

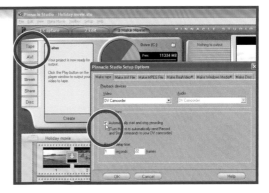

2

Oops. Sooner or later, it had to happen: we've run out of disk space. The problem is precipitated here because Studio has to render our movie as a huge DV AVI file during rendering rather than converting it to a more compressed format. Our only option is to delete some files to make space. This done, Studio gets on with the business of rendering the movie.

3

When Studio tells you that the project is ready for output, rendering is complete. Click Play in the preview window. This kick-starts the camcorder into recording mode. The movie plays back in Studio after the initial delay specified in Step 1.

4

You can monitor the recording in the camcorder's viewfinder or LCD screen. When the movie has played in its entirety, Studio instructs the camcorder to stop recording. You now have a fully rendered DV AVI movie on the MiniDV tape in your camcorder. Transfer it to VHS tape using your camcorder's analogue output and enjoy your movie the old fashioned non-digital way.

PART **8** DIGITAL VIDEO MANUAL
Burning discs

PART  Easy DVD

We'll look at DVD menus and other advanced features in the next section but what if you just want to get your finished movie onto disc with the minimum hassle? No problem: Studio will burn you a VCD, SVCD or DVD disc that will play the movie just as soon as you pop it in a DVD player. It couldn't be easier.

1

Open the Make Movie module and click the Disc tab. Now click the Settings button. Put a blank CD or DVD in the writer drive and close any 'what do you want to do' popup windows.

2

On the left, three options: VCD, SVCD and DVD. Check the appropriate option. Immediately to the right are configuration options where you can tweak the SVCD and DVD settings (but not VCD) to squeeze more video onto a single disc. For instance, with SVCD in custom mode, you can get between 32 and 39 minutes of video per CD, depending on the bit rate.

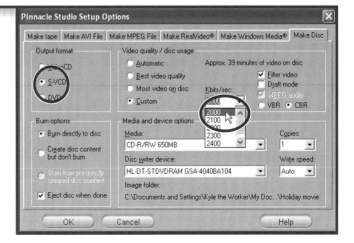

3

Check the Burn directly to disc box. Now specify what type of media you are using – a 650 or 700MB CD for a VCD or SVCD project, or any format of recordable/rewriteable DVD for a DVD project – and tell Studio which writer drive to use if there's a choice.

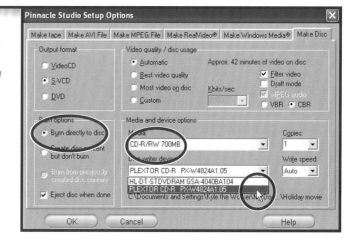

4

Click OK to start the rendering procedure. Unfortunately, here we have another oops moment. The 'diskometer' is warning us that the movie won't fit on a single disc. Now is the time to shorten the movie, or tweak the quality settings, or both.

5

That's better. Following some judicious pruning, we now have a couple of minutes to spare. Click Create disc and go and do something more interesting while Studio renders the edits, converts the video to the appropriate format (low bit rate MPEG-2 for SVCD in this example), and burns the disc. Play it in your DVD player or in a software player on your computer to check the result.

PART 8 Making menus and choosing chapters

If you want to author a more professional-looking DVD, it should include two key elements:

- **Title/menu page** This is the opening screen that appears automatically when a disc is played in a DVD player (or computer drive). Typically, it will have a background picture that represents your movie, and often a looping soundtrack. More importantly, it will have…
- **Buttons** One for each of your movies. If you only have one movie on the disc, one button will do it; but if you have two or more movies, the viewer can select which to watch via the DVD player's remote control.

Beyond these basics, you can have sub-menus with additional content (extra movies, or perhaps a still image slideshow), a

button for every chapter point in your movie, and various soundtracks and subtitles. In the following example, we will create a title page with buttons linking to two movies. We will also make good use of chapter points. This can all be done with Studio or a similar video editor.

The thing to be clear about from the outset is the difference between scenes and chapters. Your movie is made up of consecutive screens that link together with transitions, whether hard cuts or fancy effects. These scenes are either created automatically for you during video capture, or manually during the editing process, or both. But on the finished DVD, scenes are irrelevant. The DVD player doesn't 'know' or care about how you arranged your scenes to tell a story: so far as it is concerned, there is just an entire video file to be played from start to finish.

Chapters, by contrast, are markers or break points superimposed on the movie later for the benefit of the DVD player. They may bear some relation to scenes and scene changes, but they don't have to. For instance, your first chapter could be some beach footage comprised of twenty scenes stitched together; and your second chapter might be a tour of the hotel, again comprised of numerous related scenes. By adding chapter points to separate these two key elements in your story, you make it easy for a viewer to skip through the movie from point to point with the DVD player's remote control. First, though, we need to make a menu.

You can skip through a professional movie from chapter to chapter with your DVD remote but you can do just the same with home projects, too.

Here we have an edited but not yet rendered project open in the Timeline. Click the Disc Menus tab to the right of the album to open Studio's ready-made DVD menu templates. Select one with a click to see it in the preview window. Don't worry about the text as this can be changed later. If you want motion buttons on your menu – i.e. buttons in which thumbnail-sized video clips play – select one of the templates with large rectangular buttons rather than mere arrows or icons.

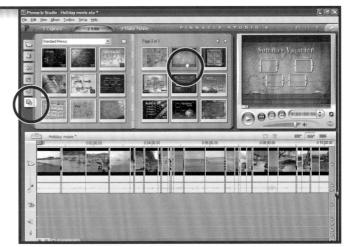

②

When you find a template that you like, or at least can bear, drag it to the video track in the Timeline and drop it onto the first scene. It immediately snaps to the beginning of the track. Studio now invites you to create chapters automatically or manually. Select the latter option and click OK.

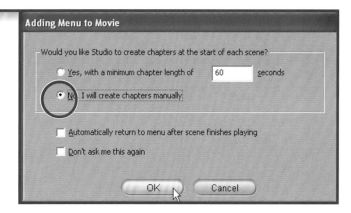

③

This opens the Clip Properties screen with the menu ripe for configuration. You now have the opportunity to split your movie into sensible chunks. The first chapter is pre-selected for you in the editing panel above the Timeline. Highlight the caption and change it to something appropriate. Here, we've opted for 'Arrival'. Check the Motion thumbnails box.

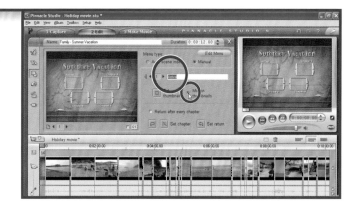

④

Use the Timeline marker or the playback controls in the preview window to locate the beginning of your first chapter. The frame field in the preview window is handy for homing in on precise frames. Your chapter point will probably coincide with the start of a clip – in this case, the first clip in the project – but it need not. When you have located and paused at the correct frame, click the Set Chapter button.

⑤

You'll see a little pink 'flag' labelled C1 appear just above the video track in the Timeline. This signifies the start of Chapter 1. The frame you selected in the previous step becomes the thumbnail for that chapter's button in the menu. If you'd rather use a more representative frame, locate it in the preview window and click the Set thumbnail button.

6

The menu changes accordingly and displays the selected frame as the chapter button. Now click the little arrows next to the chapter names field to move the selection to the next button, or simply click the relevant button in the menu itself. Here we have selected the button that relates to Chapter 2. We can rename this to anything we like.

7

As before, create a new chapter point in the Timeline and select an appropriate frame for the menu button. Continue like this throughout your movie project. When you run out of buttons on the menu – in this example, there are four – use the arrow button below the menu to turn the page, as it were.

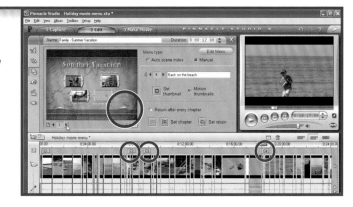

8

A couple of notes. You can drag chapter flags along the Timeline to rejig your chapter points, but remember to update button thumbnails accordingly. You can also remove a chapter point by clicking on the flag and hitting the Delete key (or by right-clicking it and selecting Delete, or by clicking the Delete chapter button). However, the menu does not redesign itself automatically. For instance, if you delete the Chapter 4 flag in the Timeline, you'll end up with a blank Chapter 4 button on the menu. Take care.

9

Note the Return after every chapter box. If you check this, as shown here, something important happens during playback. Let's say your viewer selects Chapter 2 – or 'The Old Town', as we've named it – from the menu. As soon as playback of that chapter is complete, the main menu will appear again. That is, Chapter 3 will not automatically follow on from Chapter 2 during playback. This return to the menu behaviour is represented by a left-pointing M1 flag on the Timeline.

You can have multiple menus in your project. Simply drag a new menu from the Album into the Timeline as you did in Step 2. This now becomes Menu 2, flagged on the Timeline as M2. You can now create chapter points and return to menu points for Menu 2 that control playback of the ensuing video. In this example, Menu 2 will appear on screen immediately after playback of Chapter 6. However, in order that a viewer can summon this menu directly from the main menu...

Return to Menu 1 and make Menu 2 a chapter point. This means that the viewer can access Menu 2 directly from the main menu. It's all just a matter of linking elements in your Timeline – chapter points and sub-menus – to the main menu page. For instance, your DVD could contain three distinct movies, each accessible via a button on the opening menu. Each of these movies could then have its own sub-menu with buttons linking to chapters. In fact, this would be neater than including the first movie's chapter points on the main menu. See p153 for more on this.

Now is a good time to preview how your disc will look for real. Click the DVD button under the preview window and Studio switches to a representation of a DVD player's remote control. You can see how your menus and chapters all hang together – and fix anything that doesn't. Use the arrow above the DVD button to switch to full-screen mode and the Escape key on your keyboard to return to Studio.

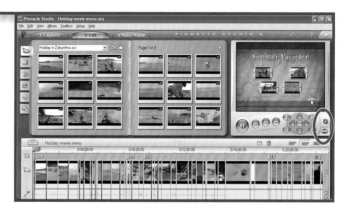

In the Timeline, menus have a duration. The default is 12 seconds. In fact, this is slightly misleading because menus always loop i.e. 'play' time and time again until the viewer makes a selection. However, you may like to have some background music accompany your menus. To do this, add a tune to the background music track (as described on p115-119). Line up the start of the track with the menu.

Now either lengthen the duration of the menu to match the music, or shorten the music to match the menu. If your music is longer than the menu, it will cut out after 12 seconds (or whatever menu duration you choose) and start again from the beginning. You have to switch to DVD preview mode (Step 13) to see and hear this behaviour. So, if you want a three-minute song to play in its entirety, make your menu three minutes' long. The viewer can cut it short at any time by selecting a button. Better, set both menu and music to, say, thirty seconds and edit the track to a thirty-second clip that loops smoothly or fades in and out.

At any time, right-click a menu in the Timeline and select Clip Properties to return to the view we saw in Step 3. You can also get here by double-clicking the menu in the Timeline. Now click the Edit Menu button top right. This opens the (hopefully) familiar screen in which you can tweak your menu design just as easily as you edited titles and captions earlier.

For instance, you can change the title text, edit the button size, style and position, and even add your own custom background. In fact, you can completely change the design of the menu safe in the knowledge that the links and functions will be preserved intact. This is the time to treat your chosen template as a starting point and tweak it to perfection. Again, check your work by using the DVD button in the preview window.

On now to burning the disc. Choose your format (VCD, SVCD or DVD), pop a blank disc in the drive, and wait an age for Studio to perform rendering, MPEG conversion and disc burning. Some time later, you'll emerge with a playable menu-driven disc. Congratulations!

BURNING DISCS

More on menus

There are several ways to build a successful DVD menu with Studio and similar video editors. But working in Timeline view isn't necessarily the easiest way to picture what's going on. You may find it helps to sketch out your menu links before you begin. Here are some examples.

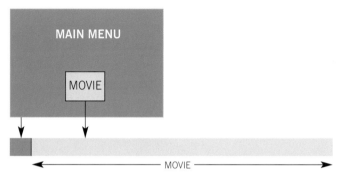

Single movie – simple
The main menu displays the movie title and a single button starts playback.

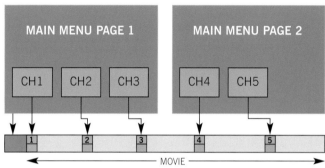

Single movie – with chapters
This time, we have added chapter points that span several pages. We did not include 'return to menu' markers so Chapter 2 will play immediately after Chapter 1, and so on. The viewer need only click the Chapter 1 button to watch the entire movie but also has the option of skipping straight to any particular chapter.

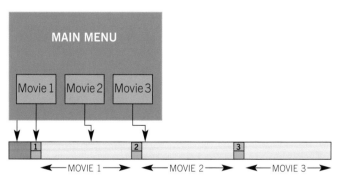

Multiple movies – simple
Here we have three movie projects on the same DVD. Each has its own button on the main menu page and can be played back directly from here. This technique is particularly useful when you already have earlier movie projects saved as disc-compatible MPEG files (p141). All you would do is open a new project in Studio, add your finished (edited, rendered and encoded) movies to the Timeline, and create a main menu that links them together as chapters.

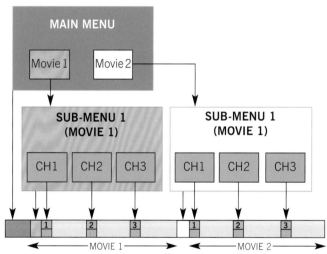

Multiple movies – with chapters
In this example, we have two movies but each has its own chapters and so requires its own menu. The viewer thus makes an initial selection from the main menu – movie 2, say – and this takes them to a sub-menu page with chapter points for that movie. The root/title menu button on the DVD player's remote returns the viewer to the main menu at any time.

The difference here is that you need to incorporate sub-menus in the project, but we've already seen how to create them (p151). The trick is then making each a chapter point in the main menu.

PART 8

Advanced authoring

We can't possibly do justice to the possibilities of DVD authoring in the space remaining. However, we must at least point out some options worth considering. Here are two.

Standalone DVD tools

Video editors are superb at what they do, which is to say editing movie projects. We've seen the benefits throughout this manual. However, disc authoring has traditionally been tacked on as an afterthought, with the result that many video editors can (or certainly could) produce only very basic VCD, SVCD and DVD discs. But disc authoring is actually a complex business with all sorts of opportunities for creativity. For instance, you might want to add subtitles in different languages, or include copy protection to prevent your movie getting ripped off, or use surround sound, or produce 16:9 widescreen movies.

Moreover, instead of working with a Studio-style Timeline, you usually get to start with a blank DVD template. You can then design your disc by creating menus from scratch, adding sub-menus wherever you need them, dragging and dropping clips and buttons, and specifying which elements link to which others. You may find this a more intuitive way of working.

If you want to try your hand with a standalone disc author, the best approach is to edit your movie in your favourite video editor and save it as a compatible video file (i.e. MPEG-1 for VCD; MPEG-2 for SVCD and DVD). While most disc authoring programs can actually do their own file format conversions, in our experience they make a pretty poor job of it. Disc authors sometimes even capture and (roughly) edit footage direct from a digital camcorder but again you should use a fully featured video editor to make a polished movie.

This is Ulead DVD Workshop 2, one of several similar programs that lets you construct a DVD (or VCD/SVCD) via an intuitive design-led interface. Correctly formatted videos can be dragged and dropped into place, and links between movies, menus and chapters are created and maintained automatically.

A basic DVD menu maker and recorder like Roxio DVD Builder can do its own MPEG-2 encoding from captured or imported video files, but frankly we don't recommend it. Look to a dedicated tool like TMPGEnc (see Appendix 1).

External encoding

However, not all MPEG encoders are alike. While Studio and VideoStudio, for example, can both produce disc-compliant MPEG-1 and MPEG-2 files, they do so in different ways and with different techniques. In fact, if you were to capture a single clip of digital video from your camcorder and convert it directly in Studio and VideoStudio as an MPEG-2 file, you would end up with files that were different in size and appearance. Which one is better is less important (and largely a subjective judgement) than whether you could achieve an altogether superior MPEG-2 file – and hence DVD – if you encode the video in a specialist application. Our experience is that you can.

We don't think it's worthwhile bothering with an external encoder for VCD and SVCD projects, and nor would we suggest it when your source is anything other than high quality video captured from a digital camcorder. Furthermore, if you're happy with your video editor's output, you may prefer to leave well alone. But if you want to try encoding your edited movie in a separate operation, here's what to do:

- Render and save the movie as a DV AVI file, as described on p142.
- Import this as the source file in your encoder program, and save the output as a DVD-compliant MPEG-2 file.
- Import this MPEG-2 file into your video editor or a standalone disc author, and burn it to disc.

And so...

Just to summarise, then, these are your options:

	Capture/edit/render	Convert to MPEG	Make disc
1	Editor	Editor	Editor
2	Editor	Editor	Author
3	Editor	Author	Author
4	Author	Author	Author
5	Editor	Encoder	Editor
6	Editor	Encoder	Author

Of these, we have looked most closely at option 1 in this manual. Editing video – i.e. using raw footage to tell a coherent story – is the trickiest but certainly the most crucial and ultimately rewarding stage in the process. In this last section, we hope to have demonstrated that a fully-featured video editor like Studio can also produce professional-looking discs. However, as time goes on, you may well wish to take full control over your disc presentations, in which case option 2 will appeal. Options 3 and 4 we don't recommend at all, as you'll sacrifice either video quality or editing flexibility or both. Option 5 introduces the notion of an external MPEG encoder, which means rendering your project in the video editor, saving it as a DV AVI file, converting it to MPEG-2 elsewhere, and then returning to the editor to make a DVD. Option 6 goes further by suggesting you take your externally encoded MPEG video file to a dedicated disc authoring program instead. This means using three programs to do a job that Studio or VideoStudio can do alone, but you get the benefit of specialist applications. This, we suspect, is where you may well end up.

We look at working with one popular MPEG encoder in Appendix 1. In Appendix 2, we consider an alternative method of converting files and burning discs that bypasses the VCD, SVCD and DVD formats completely. And finally, in Appendix 3, we consider an altogether automated approach to movie-making.

PART **9** **Appendices**

PART 9

Appendix 1 – Encoding MPEG files

On ppX-Y, we mentioned the possibility of saving an edited movie project as a DV AVI file i.e. in the same high quality format as source video captured from a digital camcorder. This gives you all the movie-making benefits of a video editor but leaves MPEG conversion (and disc authoring) for later. Here we'll work through encoding such a file in a format suitable for burning to disc.

TMPGEnc 3.0 XPress is one of many digital video programs that you simply won't find on the supermarket shelves. While Pinnacle, Ulead, Roxio and others have the consumer market pretty well stitched up, the likes of this utility are generally distributed over the internet. Not to put too fine a point on it, TMPGEnc was developed and distributed by video geeks for video geeks. The only reason that we're talking about it at all is because the latest version (at the time of writing) includes a user-friendly wizard. It remains at heart a stunningly complex tool but you can now use its main features with just a few clicks.

 Given that you already have a video editor that's perfectly capable of converting DV AVI to MPEG-1 or MPEG-2, the obvious question is: why not use it? The answer is that TMPGEnc does MPEG encoding better. It also, in our experience, takes considerably longer. So is it sufficiently better and not too much slower to merit an outlay of around $58? Perhaps. The only way to find out if you personally appreciate the difference is by trying it out for yourself. Here's how.

Download and install a 14-day trial version of TMPGEnc 3.0 XPress from **www.pegasys-inc.com/en/index.html**. *This works for 14 days and allows you to try out all the features without a commitment. Note that you must have an open internet connection in order to 'validate' the trial program licence first time around (a thoroughly daft idea that may require tweaking your firewall).*

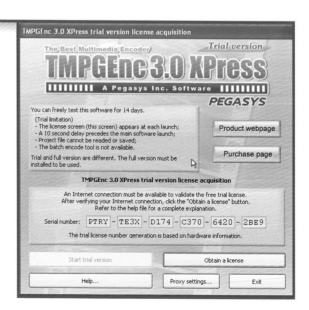

2

Meanwhile, render a sample movie – make it a short one – in your video editor and save it as a DV AVI file. In TMPGEnc, start a new project and navigate to the file. It opens in the Clip Info dialogue box. Check that the aspect ratio matches your file – in this example, the video was shot and rendered as 4:3 – and that the interlaced/progressive field matches your camcorder's setting. In most cases, your footage will be interlaced.

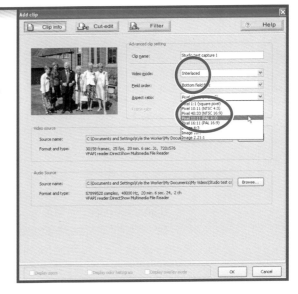

3

Click the Cut-edit button and you'll find that you can trim your movie. This would be handy if you were working with freshly captured video but here we're assuming that you've already finished your project in a video editor.

4

In the Filter page, you can do all manner of wonderful things with your video, including trimming bits off the top, bottom or edges (something you can't do in Studio) and playing around with the colours and sharpness. Again, though, we are not really concerned with such options here. Click OK to continue and open the Set Output page.

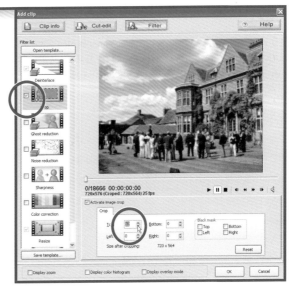

5

Lots of lovely templates. Pick the one that matches your project. We want to make a DVD-compliant MPEG-2 file in the PAL format so we've selected the appropriate template. Even here, though, you can tweak the settings. Select Linear PCM audio and ensure that VBR is selected (it takes longer because TMPGEnc has to analyse the video twice but the results are superior). Match the output aspect ratio to the source.

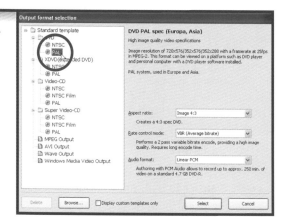

6

When you click Select to continue, you get the chance to determine the quality settings. Keep an eye on the bottom of the screen, as this shows you what proportion of a blank DVD your finished video will require. In this screenshot, the average bit rate will be 8,000Kbps, which equates to just over 20% of the disc's capacity.

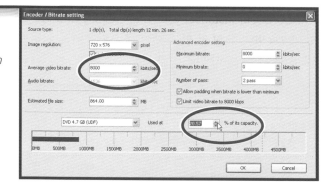

7

Click OK, open the Encode page, and specify a file name and folder location for the new video. Now click Start Output. TMPGEnc gets to work and slowly (very slowly – speed is not its strong suit) analyses and encodes the video. When it's through, you can import the MPEG-2 file into a disc authoring program or back into a video editor, ready for burning without requiring any further encoding.

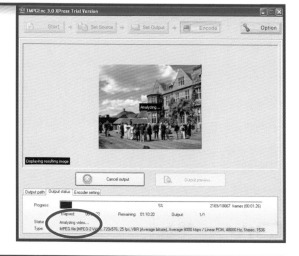

8

You can of course preview your finished video in a software player on your computer but it's worth burning it to disc, playing it in your DVD player and watching it on a television screen to better judge the effect of TMPGEnc encoding. Compare the same short movie encoded with your video editor and TMPGEnc. If you see no discernible improvement, stick with the editor's encoder.

PART **9**

Appendix 2 –
Doing it with DivX

DivX (www.divx.com) is a flexible video compression codec based on the MPEG-4 specification. Although originally developed to make it easier to distribute movies on the internet, it can also be used to produce near-DVD quality video with significantly smaller file sizes than is possible with MPEG-2. For instance, you can generally fit a full-length movie on one or at most two CDs, or squeeze several movies onto a single DVD.

Until fairly recently you could only play a DivX video on a computer. This lacks the obvious appeal of being able to watch movies on a television set. However, several manufacturers now make DivX-compatible DVD players that can play DivX discs just like regular DVDs.

Importantly, a DivX disc is quite different to a VCD, SVCD or DVD. The latter three formats all have to be properly 'authored', as we have seen i.e. you can't just copy a video file to disc and expect it to play. But this is precisely what you can do with DivX and a compatible player. A DivX disc (CD or DVD – it doesn't matter which) is simply a data disc with one or more video files on it. The one notable disadvantage is that you don't get DVD-style menus and chapter points.

The upshot is that you can convert an edited movie project into a relatively small DivX-encoded file, burn it to a CD or a DVD with any recording software (even Windows XP's built-in CD recording utility), and play it in a DivX-compatible DVD player. Specialist DVD authoring is not required. With the codec's impressive flexibility, you can also tailor progressively lower quality versions of a video for internet streaming or email attachments.

The DivX codec is free to download. Once installed on your computer, the idea is that you instruct your usual video editor or video encoder to save your movie as an AVI file encoded with the DivX codec. Unfortunately, it's not always plain sailing. We found that Studio balks at using DivX – it appeared not to support the codec as a valid encoder for AVI files, despite listing it as an option – whereas VideoStudio is happy to use DivX. So indeed is TMPGEnc (see Appendix 1).

Another option is to use a standalone DivX encoder. Dr. DivX (www.divx.com/divx/drdivx) is easy but costs $50 after a 15-day trial period; VirtualDub (www.virtualdub.org) is free, but complex.

A DivX-compatible DVD player handles DivX video files as easily as a correctly authored DVD.

Tweak the DivX codec to balance quality with file size.

Making DivX movies the Dr DivX way.

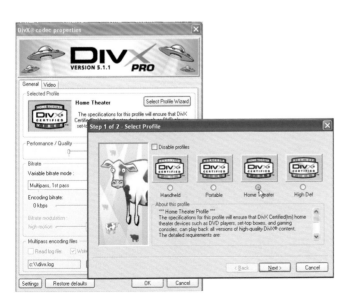

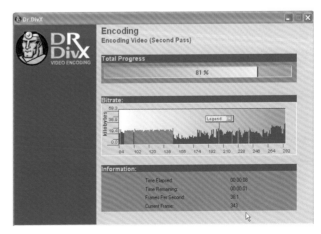

Appendix 3 – Making Muvees

And now for something completely different. Thus far, we've been looking at hands-on storyboard and timeline control with non-linear video editors, which is precisely the approach you need to adopt to structure a story. But you don't necessarily want to tell a story at all, or at least not in a conventional manner. Perhaps you just want to capture the essence of an experience, be it a sporting event, a holiday, or the kids playing in the garden. Perhaps you don't need a strict beginning–middle–end chronology. Perhaps you're frustrated with your own inability to bring footage to life and would like to see someone else have a go (even a machine). Or perhaps you're just pushed for time and want to get results with minimal effort.

As it happens, several standard video editors offer auto-movie features that attempt to take the movie-making reins. We are not inclined to recommend any of them. We are, however, rather taken with a program called Muvee autoProducer magicMoments (which we'll just call Muvee from now on). This is available from **www.muvee.com**. It costs £69.95 but there's a free trial version available.

The idea is that you feed Muvee a video or capture footage directly from a camcorder, then choose a theme and a soundtrack and let Muvee make its own movie relatively unrestricted by logic or order. It's an idea that admittedly won't appeal to many – and we were deeply sceptical – but in fact Muvee is highly effective and quite compelling.

Note that we're skipping all the background technology (or marketing pitch – we're not sure which) about "editing grammar" and "emotional index", partly because we don't understand it and partly because we don't care. What matters is whether Muvee works.

It does. Here's how.

Try the Muvee trial for a taste of hands-free movie editing.

1

The opening Muvee screen is straightforward, with seven big buttons. Topmost is Capture DV, a procedure we're familiar with by now. Connect your digital camcorder via FireWire and click this now if you want to capture fresh footage.

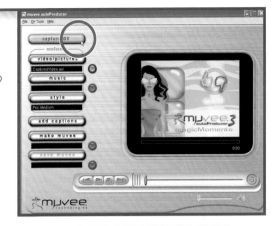

2

As with all capture programs, Muvee lets you control the camcorder remotely by means of onscreen buttons. Cue up your tape with the help of the preview window, pick a file location, give your captured video a name, and let it roll. Compared to other capture programs, we find that Muvee drops significantly more frames. Which is why...

3

You may prefer to import a pre-captured video directly into Muvee. Use the Video/Pictures button on the main page for this. On the next screen, videos that have been captured by Muvee appear to the left but you can use the Add Video button in the top right to find any other AVI or MPEG file on your computer. Select one or more and click Open.

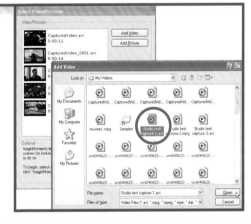

4

The newly chosen video appears in the main Video/Pictures window. Highlight it and click the magicMoments button. This is actually an optional step but one that we've found well worth taking. MagicMoments lets you preview the chosen video and determine which scenes should definitely be included in the final project and which definitely excluded.

5

First time around with a new video, Muvee has to scan it to detect and insert scene breaks, so you may find yourself stuck here for a few minutes. Eventually, you'll see the entire movie represented as a timeline. Scene divisions are flagged with white lines. Use the Play and Pause buttons (or drag the timeline marker) to watch the video. When you get to a bit that you like, click the green thumbs-up button; when you want to exclude a scene, use the red thumbs-down button. The longer you hold down the buttons, the more of that scene will be included or excluded.

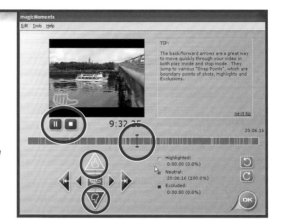

6

You can skip from one scene marker to another using the large arrow buttons to the left and right of the thumbs-up/down buttons. If you pause the video, you can also use the smaller arrow buttons to scroll back and forwards one frame at a time. You would certainly want to ditch a shot of the inside of the lens cap but the recommended strategy is to be very sparing with these manual mark-ups. Moreover, Muvee splits scenes further during composition so even an extended thumbs-down click won't necessarily exclude the whole of a lengthy scene. Don't spend too much time here, and click OK when you're finished.

7

Back in the main interface, click the Music button and then use Add Music to select one or more MP3, WMA or WAV files from your computer. Tracks are used in the order in which they appear from top to bottom so reorder them as you see fit. At the bottom of this screen is the audio mixer, a one-time only chance to adjust the balance between the video soundtrack and your selected music. Trial and error is the key here but Muvee makes it very easy indeed to return to a project time and time again.

8

Now the fun part. Click the Style button on the main screen and preview the built-in selection of video styles. Your selection here determines the overall look of the finished movie. Two points to note: you can purchase additional themes by following the More Styles button (internet connection required); and you can check or uncheck the important 'Keep shots in sequence' button. Uncheck this only if you don't mind the scene order of your footage being jumbled up (which, given that you're not trying to tell a story as such, should be just fine).

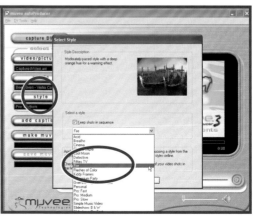

The Captions button lets you add credits fore and aft of your movie, and that's it: no fancy titling effects here. By default, you get Muvee credits but you can change these to your own. We suggest leaving the font choice to Muvee as it chooses one to fit the theme.

Now click the Make Muvee button. If you check the Manual option, and we strongly suggest that you do, you can tell Muvee how long you want your movie to be and whether or not it may repeat scenes or music tracks. Finally, click Continue and sit back for a while as Muvee completes its analysis and makes a movie.

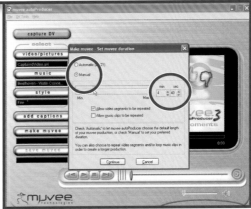

Use the onscreen transport controls to watch your finished production. At this point, you can go back and change any of the options – sound, captions, theme etc. – and Muvee will knock up a new version in just a few moments. First time out is always the longest because that's when the analysis gets done. We suggest you save the project now from the File menu.

When you're happy with your movie, use the Save Muvee button to save it in the file format of your choice. Muvee offers the full range, from streaming web video to high quality DVD. You can even burn the movie directly to disc if you have a CD or DVD writer, but only if Muvee finds a supported recording program. We reckon it's best leaving disc authoring to a dedicated tool and recommend that you simply save your movie to the hard disk here. Bear in mind that you can also import a finished and saved Muvee video into Studio or another conventional video editor for use in a wider project. You might, for instance, use Muvee to jazz up your stag-weekend-in-Amsterdam footage and include this as a comedy segment in your wedding video.

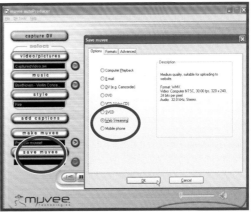

Index

ACKNOWLEDGEMENTS

Author	**Kyle MacRae**
Copy Editor	**Shena Deuchars**
Page build	**James Robertson**
Photography	**Iain McLean**
	Paul Buckland
Index	**Nigel d'Auvergne**
Project Manager	**Louise McIntyre**

Thanks to Jessops in Yeovil for the loan of equipment
for Chapter opener images